The
FRENCH
WAY

6°   4°   2°   0°   2°   4°   6°   8°

MER DU NORD

PAYS-BAS

GRANDE-BRETAGNE

ALLEMAGNE

52°

Calais
Dunkerque
Lille
BELGIQUE

LUXEMBOURG

50°

MANCHE

Cherbourg
Dieppe
Amiens   St. Quentin
Le Havre
Rouen
Reims
Caen
Seine   Paris   Marne   Metz
Roscoff   Meuse
Brest   St.-Malo   Nancy
St-Brieuc   Strasbourg
Quimper   Seine
Fontainebleau   Troyes   Colmar
Rennes   Le Mans   Rhin
Lorient   Orléans   Mulhouse
Saône   Belfort
St. Nazaire   Angers   Tours   Dijon   Besançon
Nantes
Châteauroux   Bourges   Nevers
Poiters   Saône
Moulins
La Rochelle   FRANCE   Montluçon   Mâcon   SUISSE
Royan   Cognac   Limoges   Clermont-Ferrand   Lyon
Angoulême   Rhône
OCÉAN ATLANTIQUE   MASSIF CENTRAL   St. Étienne
Périgueux   Brive-la-Gaillarde   Grenoble
Bordeaux   Dordogne   Le Puy   Valence   ITALIE
Bergerac   Figeac
Arcachon   Cahors   Espalion   Gap
Agen   Aveyron   Mende   Rhône
Garonne   Millau   Alès
Montauban   Avignon   Nice
Biarritz   Dax   Nîmes   Aix-en-Provence   Cannes
Bayonne   Mirande   Toulouse   Béziers   Montpellier
Pau   Tarbes   Garonne   Narbonne   Marseille
ESPANGE   Lourdes   Carcassonne   Toulon
PYRÉNÉES   Perpignan   MER MÉDITERRANÉE

52°

50°

48°

46°

44°

CORSE
Bastia
Ajaccio
Porto-Vecchio

0   50   100   150   200 Miles
0   50   100   150   200   250   300 Kilometres

FRANCE

The FRENCH WAY

Aspects of Behavior,

Attitudes, and Customs

of the French

ROSS STEELE

PASSPORT BOOKS

NTC/Contemporary Publishing Group

cover photos
Courtesy of French Tourist Organization (top left, bottom left, and top right)
Photos by David Simson (middle left, middle right, and bottom right)

Published by Passport Books
An imprint of NTC/Contemporary Publishing Company
4255 West Touhy Avenue, Lincolnwood (Chicago), Illinois 60646-1975 U.S.A.
Copyright © 1995 by Passport Books
Printed in the United States of America
International Standard Book Number: 0-8442-1495-7
  8 9 VP 9 8 7 6 5

Contents

Introduction   ix

1. Abbreviations and acronyms   1
2. Accents and language   3
3. Americanization   5
4. Anglo-Saxon   6
5. Animals   7
6. **Bleu-blanc-rouge**   7
7. Bourgeoisie   8
8. Bread and pastries   9
9. Bridges and tunnels   10
10. Business   11
11. **Cafés**   13
12. Calling cards   14
13. Chic and designer luxury goods   15
14. Cinema   15
15. **Cocorico!**   16
16. Conversation   17
17. Cultural tourism   18
18. Culture   19
19. Decorations   20
20. Documents and forms   20
21. Drinking   21
22. Driving   22

CONTENTS

23. Ecology   23
24. Education   24
25. Europe   26
26. **Extra!**   28
27. Family   29
28. Fashion   29
29. Flowers and gardens   31
30. Friendship   31
31. Frogs and snails, garlic and truffles   32
32. Gambling   32
33. Gastronomy and restaurants   33
34. Gendarmes and demonstrations   35
35. Gestures   36
36. Government and politics   37
37. **Grandeur**   38
38. Greetings and farewells   39
39. Guillotine   41
40. Health and fitness   41
41. Heroes and heroines   42
42. Hexagon   44
43. High tech   44
44. Holidays   46
45. Housing   48
46. Humor   50
47. Immigration   51
48. **Je t'aime**   52
49. **Joie de vivre**   53
50. Kilos   53
51. Kissing   54
52. Leisure   55
53. **Liberté, égalité, fraternité**   56
54. Logic   56
55. Marriage and divorce   57
56. **La Marseillaise**   58
57. Meals   59
58. Media   60
59. Men and women   61
60. Money   63

61. Names and name days   64
62. Numbers   65
63. Overseas departments and territories   66
64. Paris   68
65. Parisians   70
66. Politeness and directness   71
67. **Queues** (Lines)   72
68. Regionalization   72
69. Religion   74
70. Republic   75
71. Rights   77
72. Shopping   78
73. Sports   79
74. Street names and addresses   81
75. Time   82
76. Transport   83
77. Urban and rural life   84
78. Vacations   85
79. Work and unemployment   87
80. World wars and colonial wars   88
81. X   89
82. Xenophobia   90
83. **Yéyé**   91
84. Zapping   91
85. **Zut!**   92

Bibliography   93

Index   95

INTRODUCTION

France's cities, villages, and picturesque countryside, her medieval cathedrals, castles, and art museums, her restaurants, high-fashion, and luxury goods are well known throughout the world. But who are the French? Foreigners have many different views of them, both positive and negative.

This book presents a portrait of today's French society through some characteristic French behaviors, attitudes, and customs. During recent times, many traditional French values have been buffeted by the winds of change, which have produced deep tensions within the social groups caught up in the process of modernization, the greater influence of the European Union on daily life, and the globalization of economic forces. The tension between nationalism and internationalism, for example, has erupted onto the world stage as France has adopted an independent position in political and economic negotiations aimed at increasing cooperation between nations. This has led to criticisms of French arrogance. On the other hand, France has consistently pursued a policy of promoting world peace, humanitarian aid through **Médecins sans Frontières** (Doctors without Borders), and economic aid programs by wealthy nations in developing countries.

Foreigners looking at France from the viewpoint of their own cultural values often misunderstand French reactions and perceive contradictions in the collective behavior of the French. This book helps to clear up such misunderstandings by placing French behavior and attitudes in their own context and explaining why longstanding traditions within France give coherence to French reactions when seen from within their society. Readers will acquire greater awareness of similarities and differences between their cultural traditions and those of France. This increased knowledge will increase their capacity to communicate appropriately with the French and enjoy their company. On a personal level, the French can be the most charming of acquaintances and the most loyal of friends. Above all, they are individuals in a country where individualism is a national characteristic.

Alexis de Tocqueville wrote in 1865 that "The French are at once the most brilliant and the most dangerous of all European nations, and the best qualified to become, in the eyes of other peoples, an object of admiration, of hatred, of compassion, or alarm—never of indifference." Many foreigners today still share this opinion. The French continue to surprise, frustrate, amuse, and stimulate the world.

1. ABBREVIATIONS AND ACRONYMS

Abbreviations have entered the daily vocabulary of the French. Tourists will need to recognize these:

Transport

RATP **Régie autonome des transports parisiens**
Autonomous administration of Parisian transportation; the Paris metro and bus system

RER **Réseau Express Régional**
Paris regional rapid rail transport system

SNCF **Société Nationale des Chemins de Fer Français**
National syndicate of railroads; the national train system

TEE **Trans-Europe-Express**
Trans-Europe express train

TGV **Train à grande vitesse**
High-speed train

VAL **Véhicule automatique léger**
Light automatic vehicle; driverless metro train

European and International Institutions

ALENA **Accord de libre-échange nord américain**
North American Free Trade Agreement (NAFTA)

CEE	**Communauté économique européenne** the European Economic Community
EURO	**Unité monétaire européenne** European currency unit
GATT	**Accord général sur les tarifs douaniers et le commerce** General Agreement on Tariffs and Trade
ONU	**Organisation des Nations Unies** the United Nations Organization
OTAN	**Organisation du Traité de l'Atlantique du Nord** North Atlantic Treaty Organization (NATO)
SME	**Système monétaire européen** European monetary system
UE	**Union européenne** the European Union

French Institutions

ANPE	**Agence nationale pour l'emploi** the national unemployment agency
BNP	**Banque nationale de Paris** National Bank of Paris, a major national bank
EDF	**Electricité de France** the state-owned electricity agency
GDF	**Gaz de France** the state-owned natural gas agency
P et T or **PTT**	**Postes et télécommunications** or **Postes, télégraphes et téléphones** the French post office and telephone monopoly

Daily Life

BCBG	**Bon chic, bon genre** typical appearance of the young bourgeois yuppie

BD **Bande dessinée**
a cartoon or comic book; literally, "drawn strip"

CRS **Compagnies Républicaines de Sécurité**
Republican Companies of Safety; the riot police

FNAC **Fédération Nationale des Achats des Cadres**
discount chain of book, record, and computer stores

HLM **Habitations à loyer modéré**
low-rent dwellings, cheap high-rise housing condominiums

PDG **Président-directeur général**
CEO of a firm

PMU **Pari mutuel urbain**
the state horse-race betting agency

PV **Procès verbal (Contravention)**
parking fine

SDF **Sans domicile fixe**
without definite residence; homeless

SIDA **Syndrome d'immunodéficience acquise**
AIDS

SVP **s'il vous plaît**
please

TVA **Taxe sur la valeur ajoutée**
value-added tax

2. ACCENTS AND LANGUAGE

French is spoken with a different accent in different parts of France. The rapid, taut Parisian accent is very different from the twangy, nasal accent in the South of France, which—if we are to believe the Southerners—reflects their jovial personality and their sunny climate.

As in all languages, the spoken language evolves more rapidly than the written language. Cardinal Richelieu (1585–1642) established the **Académie française** in 1635 to stabilize and perfect the French language. Today you will hear many colloquial and slang ex-

3

pressions that the forty elected-for-life members of the **Académie française** refuse to include in their dictionary, which rules over the correctness of the French language. Many words in French have a Greek or Latin origin. Greek or Latin roots frequently combine with Greek or Latin prefixes and suffixes to coin new French words, for example **autoroute, télévision.**

Generally the French have a conservative attitude toward the written language and take pride in their knowledge of its complexities. A majority of French people have opposed recent official attempts to modernize spelling. A highly popular national competition shown on television selects the best speller in a test of words whose spelling is made even more difficult by gender and grammatical agreements.

The first English word to enter the French language was *acre* in 1125. Since then the French have borrowed many English words, but their pronunciation and often their meaning have changed—English speakers don't always recognize them in French conversation. The number of borrowed English words has increased greatly in recent decades as a result of the rapid growth of American technology, computerization, and business management practices.

The language of France has always been **une affaire d'État** (a state affair). Alarmed by the lack of precision in usage and the loss of the "purity" of the French language that resulted from borrowed Anglo-American words and syntax, the government in 1966 established the **Haut Comité de la Langue Française,** a commission under the prime minister's control. Its mission was to defend French against the linguistic invasion of English by creating French words to replace English ones and to discourage the use of **franglais** (a mixture of French and English). In 1994 the French Parliament passed the Toubon law to expand similar 1975 legislation making it obligatory to give a translation of foreign words or phrases used in advertisements. The new law makes it mandatory to use the French language in all spheres of economic, social, and intellectual life and for all public notices and advertisements in France.

French is spoken as an official or major language in more than forty countries outside France by an estimated 120 million people. The accents in countries like Québec, Haïti, and Sénégal vary greatly from one another and from what one hears in France. This diversity is

4

a source of vitality for the continuing universal use of the French language.

❁

3. AMERICANIZATION

The French have for a long time been fascinated by the skyscrapers of New York, Hollywood westerns, and American business schools whose methods were seen as the key to new economic prosperity. The older generation also remembers with gratitude the bravery of the G.I.s who helped liberate France at the end of World War II. The G.I.s also, however, introduced to France certain American customs, like chewing gum, which the French see as negative influences on their traditional way of life. More recently the proliferation of Coca-Cola and fast-food outlets such as McDonald's (**McDo** in colloquial French) has provoked hostile criticism of a perceived takeover of French life by American values. In some cases, France has transformed the American institution along French lines, such as **le Drugstore,** which contains not only a pharmacy but also a newsstand, specialty shops, and trendy restaurants.

The opening of the Euro Disney theme park in 1992 at Marne-la-Vallée, thirty-two kilometers east of Paris, focused the debate on the survival of French cultural traditions against the threat of international American culture. The French government welcomed the thousands of new jobs at the park; French workers objected to the Disney organization's strict codes of dress and cultural behavior. The Disney corporate culture disallows the serving of alcoholic drinks, but French tourists are accustomed to drinking wine with their meals. Finances may in the long run decide the matter in French culture's favor, for the park has had a much lower number of visitors than it budgeted for, and Disney has conceded on the serving of alcohol to remove at least that obstacle to the solvency of its enterprise. The more basic influence of the attraction for the French public of Mickey and Minnie Mouse on Main Street USA in the center of the theme park is yet to be decided. In October 1994, Euro Disney changed its name to Disneyland Paris.

Anti-Americanism became strident in 1993. American pop and rock music, television programs, and movies came under attack, for many French people believed that importing them stifled the expression of French values and the growth of France's own creative industries. Eighty percent of French movie houses are controlled by American film distributors, and the national radio system maintains a 40 percent minimum of French songs only by government mandate. In the final round of talks on the 1993 General Agreement on Tariffs and Trade (GATT), France successfully led opposition to the American proposal to include those industries in the agreement, which would have lowered individual countries' barriers to imports of music, television programs, and films. France's successful campaign in the GATT talks means that France will maintain the right to defend itself against unwelcome colonization by American culture by continuing to subsidize its film and television industries and to impose minimum quotas on the number of French songs heard on French radio.

4. ANGLO-SAXON

The French often use the term **Anglo-Saxon** pejoratively as a collective description of all English speakers from countries strongly influenced by British culture. The centuries of rivalry between France and Great Britain for world supremacy explains negative attitudes toward the British as in the frequently used in the expression **la perfide Albion** (treacherous Britain), apparently originally used by French sailors who were disoriented by the similarity between the English cliffs of Dover and the cliffs of Calais on the French side of the Channel.

Anglo-Saxons in general and the English in particular are characterized as cold and aloof. In comparison, the latin temperament of the French is considered far superior. Americans are distinguished as a separate group among Anglo-Saxons. As a reaction against the success of American pop culture in France, the French see Americans as childlike, uncivilized, and without taste. These global stereotypes reveal more about the opinion the French have of themselves than about the peoples they caricature.

5. ANIMALS

The French are a nation of animal lovers.

The percentage of French homes with pets is the highest in Europe. One out of three homes has a dog; one out of four has a cat; one out of ten has a bird. Paris has more dogs than children. The proportion of pet-owning homes seems especially surprising given the large number of French families who live in apartments, but then French city dwellers have strong links with rural France, where pets are traditional. The German shepherd is the most popular breed of dog, followed by the poodle and the Breton spaniel. Asnières, a suburb of Paris, has a famous pet cemetery.

Brigitte Bardot (1934–   ) has campaigned for the need to protect animals (especially seals) from human cruelty, and she has established the Foundation of Animal Protection.

6. *BLEU-BLANC-ROUGE*

Blue, white, and red are the colors of the French flag, which is also called **le Tricolore** (three colors). The flag dates from the French Revolution and replaced the flag of the monarchy, which was adorned by the **fleur de lys** (lily). The lily's color, white, was the royal color and blue and red were the colors of Paris, which the Marquis de La Fayette proposed combining in the Revolutionaries' tricolor cockade to symbolize the union of the monarchy and the people. Perhaps coincidentally, these same colors were those of a sister revolutionary nation for whose establishment La Fayette had fought a few years earlier: the United States of America.

The **fleur de lys** is today the symbol of Québec and can be seen in the Québec flag and on car registration plates with the inscription **Je me souviens** (I remember [my French origins]).

French national sports teams wear blue when they compete internationally and are called **les Bleus** (the Blues).

7. BOURGEOISIE

The bourgeoisie, the middle class, grew in power and importance during the nineteenth century as a result of the 1789 Revolution, which put an end to the privileges of the nobility who had dominated French society until that time. Because membership in the true nobility depended solely on being born in that social class and not on personal merit or achievements, the Revolutionaries considered the nobility's privileges unjust.

The wealth of the nobility was shattered by the Revolution. The new wealthy class was the bourgeoisie, who provided the bankers, the traders, and the shopkeepers for the economic growth of post-Revolutionary France. In addition to their wealth, the bourgeoisie achieved social power by marrying members of the impoverished nobility. They increased the political power they had won in the 1789 Revolution by supplying the educated work force for the expanding administrative bureaucracy. The Industrial Revolution further increased their wealth and influence.

The vast French middle class has imposed its values and tastes on twentieth-century France despite opposition from two groups: the working class, which became more politically organized through trade unions and the Communist Party, and the intellectual class, which expressed its contempt for the bourgeois obsession with money and materialistic goals. The growth of the liberal professions (doctors, lawyers, etc.) and of senior management in industry and commerce expanded the top echelons of the bourgeoisie during **les trente glorieuses,** the thirty years of rapid economic growth in France after World War II. During this period, the traditional bourgeois attitude of spending little and saving as much money as possible changed under pressure from the consumer society. A generation of affluent, professionally successful men and women emerged, the "new bourgeoisie." Unlike the preceding generations, they were not afraid to use credit to purchase consumer and luxury goods that were not essential but enhanced their lifestyle. The glossy magazine sold with *Le Figaro* newspaper on Saturdays reflects the tastes and aspirations of these new trendsetters.

It has been said that in today's France the old aristocracy has given way to a new one that controls the political, economic, intellectual, and social power of the nation. This class is made up of the leaders in politics, industry, management, public administration, and the liberal professions. Their power is based on family connections, success, and wealth. Their values are conservative and nationalistic. They are **les gens bien** (the admirable people), whose attitudes, fashions, and lifestyles fascinate the lower social classes, who emulate them. The 1993 election of the patrician Édouard Balladur (1929–   ) and his Gaullist government was a new victory for the bourgeois establishment after the successes of socialist culture during the previous decade of François Mitterrand's (1916–   ) presidency. Two centuries after the Revolution a strong social hierarchy remains. However, the upper levels of the bourgeoisie have replaced the nobility at the top of the hierarchy.

❁

8. BREAD AND PASTRIES

Although bread is now sold in supermarkets, the French **boulangerie** (baker's shop) remains indispensable to the French way of life. Local bakers owe their comfortable survival to two facts, one historical and the other cultural/culinary. The historical fact is the cold disdain of Marie-Antoinette; the cultural/culinary fact is the nature of the bread itself.

Bread is heavily subsidized by the national government and remains astonishingly low in (apparent) cost. Bread retains enormous political significance in France since Marie-Antoinette's (1755–93) alleged callous reply, on being told that the people had no bread during the French Revolution, "Well, then, let them eat cake!" From 1789 to the present day, no French government would dare allow the price of bread to climb out of reach of the poorest French family.

French bread is baked fresh several times a day and must be available locally, since it stales perceptibly in a matter of hours. No French meal is complete without bread, not even breakfast, which commonly consists of nothing more than the leftover bread from the night before and a cup of chocolate or coffee. Jam or spreadable processed cheese sometimes accompanies the bread at breakfast.

The name of the long crusty French loaf indicates its thickness and weight: **la ficelle** is the thinnest; then come **la baguette** (the commonest), **la flûte,** and **le pain.** At meals the French usually break bread with their hands and eat it without butter. For lunch in a café a French loaf can be cut in half and sliced lengthwise to make **un sandwich** filled with **pâté,** cheese, or ham. The **boulangerie** also sells croissants, different types of rolls, and simple pastries like **un chausson aux pommes** (apple-filled pastry).

The French cake shop, **la pâtisserie,** may sell bread in addition to its mouth-watering range of cakes, tarts, and elaborate pastries. Many have religious or historical connotations—such as **une religieuse,** a chocolate éclair shaped to resemble a nun; **une madeleine,** a cake named after a nineteenth-century pastry cook and made famous by the novelist Marcel Proust (1871–1922), who discovered that it recalled his childhood memories; or **la tarte Tatin,** a caramelized apple tart named after restaurant owner Madame Tatin. A French schoolchild with a few francs to spend might stop at **la pâtisserie** on the way home from school to buy a **petit pain au chocolat,** a generous bun of flaky pastry with a slice of chocolate baked in the middle.

On Sunday mornings the **pâtisserie** shops do a brisk trade in cakes and fruit tarts, which are bought as a dessert for the family Sunday lunch. For weddings and christenings, a **pièce montée,** a tall cone-shaped arrangement of caramelized **profiteroles,** is the traditional pastry cake served to guests.

❁

9. BRIDGES AND TUNNELS

The ancient stone bridges across the Seine in Paris (the oldest is, ironically, the **Pont Neuf,** built between 1578 and 1604), together with the banks of the Seine, have been part of the romantic image of Paris since Maurice Chevalier's (1888–1972) famous song **"Sous les ponts de Paris"** (Under the Bridges of Paris). Another historic bridge built between 1177 and 1185 by Saint Bénézet and his disciples across the river Rhône at Avignon has also been made famous by a traditional children's song, **"Sur le pont d'Avignon"** (On the Bridge of Avignon).

Contemporary French bridges and tunnels have been used as symbols of French engineering prowess to project an international image of modern industrial France whose achievements are not limited to arts and culture. Examples are the Pont de Tancarville (1959), suspended 47 meters above the Seine in Normandy; the Pont de Normandie (1995), at the mouth of the Seine between Le Havre and Honfleur, which is as long as the Champs-Élysées in Paris and is one of the largest cable bridges in the world; the tunnel under Mont Blanc in the Alps (1965), linking France and Italy; the Euro Tunnel under the English Channel (1994) between Calais and Folkestone, which allows the super-fast TGV train to make the journey from Paris to London in three hours.

❁

10. BUSINESS

Every country has a distinctive business culture. When you arrive in an American office for a business appointment, you are offered coffee. In France you are not offered anything to drink. The American business office has a comfortable atmosphere with paintings or prints on the wall, plants, reference books, a family photograph, and a discrete nameplate on the desk facing the visitor. It is an extension of home. In France, offices are often cramped and don't have these friendly features. American male executives wear suits but will receive visitors with their jackets off. The French are more formal. They don't take their jackets off, although middle managers often wear sports coats. Americans hand over their business cards immediately. The French prefer to give out business cards at the end of a meeting.

The French begin a business negotiation with a series of general considerations and statements before getting down to the details. For example, they want to discuss the general business climate, economic trends, market conditions, and competing companies and their turn-overs before discussing the financial details of the sale or profits to be made from the proposal. Americans tend to concentrate much earlier in a conversation on the "bottom line" details of how to reduce costs and increase profits from the deal under negotiation. Americans who are used to adopting a much more pragmatic approach can find the intellectual approach of the French unsettling.

Americans also tend to proceed more rapidly to wrap up a deal and to give more importance to the details of the final written agreement, setting out strict conditions if things go wrong. The French place more value on the unwritten agreement and on the good intentions of both parties. In addition to the financial details, they need to have a good feeling about the people and company they are negotiating with and are prepared to take more on trust. They tend not to follow such strict procedures in reviewing a proposal and so may appear disorganized to Americans focused on rapid outcomes. It would be a mistake to imagine that the French behavior arises from any lack of thoroughness in checking details before reaching a decision. They simply follow different paths, which take longer and can frustrate time-conscious Americans.

French people sometimes interpret American directness as brusqueness. The French are more diplomatic. They don't like confrontation and don't like to lose face. Instead of giving a direct no, they will, for example, suggest a need for more information. Foreigners need to understand French body language in order to interpret what is not said. For the French, it's important for things to look good up front.

France has many business schools, often associated with a local chamber of commerce. The top business school is the **École des Hautes Études Commerciales (H.E.C.),** which is one of the most prestigious **Grandes Écoles.** Many senior executives in French industry and nationalized companies, however, have not attended a business school but have instead a math and science background from one of the most famous of the **Grandes Écoles,** the **École Polytechnique (X)** or the **École Nationale d'Administration (E.N.A.).** Intercompany dealings often take their cue, in fact, from the hierarchy of the school system, and a proposal may succeed largely because the negotiators attended the same **Grande École.** When the growth of consumerism and international trade in the 1960s and 1970s caused France to modernize its business culture, French students began coming to the United States to add a business diploma to their training. Americans are also going to study in Europe, with which the United States enjoys a mutually beneficial economic partnership and which shares with the United States a basically similar model of capitalism.

Golf and parties are less frequent forms of corporate entertainment in France than in the United States. The French use lunches and dinners to get to know their clients and to formalize the conclusion of an agreement. While a U.S. business person might invite a client to his or her home for an informal meal with his or her family, in France business meals take place in restaurants and conversation about family topics is infrequent. In this there is, however, a difference between Paris and the provinces, where a warmer personal relationship is established and the client may be invited to meet the executive's family.

Business activity slows down considerably during August, which is the traditional vacation month. Some industrial plants shut down, many companies maintain only skeletal staffing, and small shopkeepers in the cities hang a sign on their doors that reads **Fermé pour vacances annuelles** (Closed for annual vacation). After this national rest period, business, school, and politics begin again in September.

❁

11. *CAFÉS*

The **café** is one of the best-known symbols of French lifestyle. Open from early till late, providing food, drinks, and coffee before and after restaurants have closed, the **café** is, however, far more than a place to drink. It is a meeting place for students and friends or acquaintances. The casual **On prend un verre?** can be an invitation to continue an interesting conversation with a new acquaintance, to take a break from grueling work or a boring routine, or to explore the romantic possibilities of a chance encounter.

In the lively and densely populated environment of urban France where people don't readily invite friends home, the **café** is the place where people meet and talk. It can be somewhere to read, write, or sit on your own over a drink. More importantly, it is a public arena, open to the street (with a glass frontage in winter and chairs and tables outside in summer), where people can be seen socializing or simply watching the passing crowd.

The social importance of the **café** is reflected in its ubiquity in every French town or village. The visitor to France may notice certain universal common features. The pinball machines (**les flippers**) are played by young and old. Incidentally, the pinball machine is more a prized feature than a fixture, as it tends to be in the United States; in France it is *not* acceptable to set a drink on the glass, for example. To stand and drink at the counter (**le comptoir** or **le zinc**) costs less than to sit at a table. The hard-boiled eggs on the counters are available for quick snacks.

As casual a part of French life as the **café** is, the conventions of greeting the waiters and owners and ordering are strictly observed. Customers show their formal respect by using the **vous** forms and **Monsieur** and **Madame,** opening the exchange with a **Bonjour,** and saying **Au revoir** on leaving.

The traditional tip (**le pourboire**) for the waiter, which the customer once added as a percentage of the bill, has been officially replaced by a service charge included in the bill.

❂

12. CALLING CARDS

Calling cards and business cards (both called **cartes de visite**) are frequently used in France. Single and married people send their calling cards, printed with their names and home addresses, instead of commercial greeting cards when issuing invitations and expressing New Year wishes. Incidentally, it is more traditional in France to send New Year greetings, throughout January, rather than Christmas greetings, although Christmas cards appear in shops more often than formerly.

People use a formal style in the messages on their calling cards, which means in part avoiding the use of *I* or *we.* An example would be **M. et Mme Jacques Beaumarchais vous souhaitent une très heureuse Nouvelle Année** (Mr. and Mrs. Jacques Beaumarchais wish you a very happy New Year).

Business cards are used much as they are in the United States, although perhaps a little more frequently, in a somewhat wider variety of circumstances, and by a rather wider range of occupations.

A **faire-part** is a different sort of card, printed as the occasion demands, to announce births, marriages, and deaths. A **faire-part** to announce a marriage is sent in the names not only of the parents of the bride but also of all her surviving grandparents. *Le Figaro,* a national daily with a mainly bourgeois readership, prints a special page called *Le Carnet du Jour* (The Daily Notebook) that carries various kinds of **faire-part.**

❂

13. CHIC AND DESIGNER LUXURY GOODS

French luxury goods have contributed much to the world's traditional image of France. A French origin gives a cachet to high fashion clothes, perfumes carrying the names of leading fashion designers, Hermès silk scarves, Cartier watches and jewelry, Louis Vuitton luggage, Baccarat crystal, vintage wines, cognac, and champagne. Armagnac may be somewhat finer than American applejack, but surely the French origin of Armagnac accounts for much of the difference in price. French brands command more than half of the world's luxury goods market.

The French reputation is not unearned. French luxury products benefit from expertise in craft and design accumulated over centuries and from the priority on aesthetic rather than utilitarian principles that the French have maintained. French expertise has not, however, made French markets impregnable to designers of other countries. The pyramidal glass entrance to the Louvre museum, a spectacular and successful combination of the ancient and the modern added in 1989 during bicentenary celebrations of the Revolution, was designed by the Chinese-American architect I. M. Pei (1917–   ).

❂

14. CINEMA

The Cannes Film Festival, which began in 1946, attracts much international attention in May each year with its **Palme d'Or** (Golden Palm) award for the best film and with its other awards for the best director and actors.

Paris was the site of the first public commercial screening of films. The Lumière brothers, Auguste (1862–1954) and Louis (1864–1948), presented eleven two-minute films, one of which was *La*

Sortie des usines Lumière ([Workers] Exiting the Lumière [photographic materials] Factory).

French cinema has an international reputation, which it has earned particularly for its art films and for its cinema theorists who write for *Les Cahiers du cinéma.* To encourage the production of French movies, the government subsidizes the cinema industry through a tax on ticket sales.

In the French tradition, films are better known for their directors than the actors featured in them. The French director is an author, like a novelist, who makes films in his or her own distinctive style and over which he or she has complete creative control. This contrasts directly with the American Hollywood film tradition, which promotes leading actors rather than directors. The best-known movie actors in France currently are Catherine Deneuve (1943–   ) and Gérard Dépardieu (1948–   ). Famous examples of directors in the French tradition are Jean Renoir (1894–1979), René Clair (1898–1981), Louis Malle (1932–95), François Truffaut (1932–84), and Agnès Varda (1928–   ).

The French movie industry did not adopt the Hollywood-formula blockbuster or musical comedy with spectacular dancing. It concentrates on more intellectual and psychological themes in its films, and love relationships are a frequent theme.

Going to the movies is a very popular pastime in France, and conversations among friends frequently have recent movies as a topic. French audiences enjoy Hollywood westerns and their own home-grown slapstick satirical comedies and historical dramas.

❁

15. *COCORICO!*

The crow of the rooster in France is **cocorico,** not cock-a-doodle-doo as in English. A French dog's bark is **ouah! ouah!** and a French cat's mew is **miaou.**

As the eagle is an emblem of the United States, the rooster **(le coq gaulois)** is an emblem of France. This emblem symbolizes vigilance and arose in the middle of the seventeenth century when an official French medal depicted a rooster chasing away the Spanish lion. France's enemies, in reaction, began to caricature France as a rooster. France adopted the rooster as its official emblem, used on the flagstaff of its army regiments, during the July monarchy and the Second Republic (1830–52). The seal of the French Republic since 1848 shows the allegorical Liberty seated at a rudder that is decorated with a rooster. French sports teams use the rooster as their emblem in international competitions.

French parodists and cartoonists use **le coq gaulois** and its **cocorico** to lampoon proud French nationalism and chauvinism. If one French person is seen as boasting too much about personal successes, another person in the group is liable to deride the behavior with a **cocorico!**

The rooster on the bell towers of French churches has another history. It represents only the rooster whose crow greets the dawn each day. The militantly secular government of the 1789 Revolution confiscated church property, removed the crosses from the church bell towers that dominated village skylines, and replaced the crosses with roosters.

❁

16. CONVERSATION

The French attach special importance to conversation, which they consider a skill that can be learned and developed to the level of an art. The literary salons of the seventeenth and eighteenth century established the rules of the art. Women of intellect and sophistication presided over the salons, for example the Marquise de Pompadour (1721–64), King Louis XV's (1710–74) official mistress, in whose salon philosophers and artists gathered to discuss the new theories and ideas of the Age of Enlightenment.

Modern French conversations center on general topics of social and cultural interest and offer the participants an opportunity to exchange ideas and opinions. French people, even in a very relaxed gathering, rarely talk about the weather and even more rarely about money or events at work. Food and politics are common topics in what is usually a general discussion in which everyone is expected to voice an opinion. One reason for this is that from an early age, schoolchildren are taught to reason and to analyze a topic from different points of view.

An Anglo-Saxon observing French people in conversation is often struck by the fact that they speak loudly, interrupt each other continually, argue intensely to the point where it seems they will be enemies forever, and then the discussion subsides and everyone is smiling and at ease with each other. Why? Because all the participants are expected to express their opinions frankly and to defend them when someone disagrees. Intelligent disagreement can be one of the main pleasures of conversation, even between closest friends.

Some foreigners would claim that the French prefer discussion to action. One anonymous Anglo-Saxon businessman, impatient with the delays in acting on a decision because of the French need to discuss its principles, parodied the French attitude as "it sounds all right in practice, but how does it work in theory?" The long discussion time about the abstract principles of a project is characteristic of a people whose ideals are intellectual rather than pragmatic.

❁

17. CULTURAL TOURISM

Not all the tourists who flock to France's museums, galleries, castles, cathedrals, and churches pass through French customs; many are French themselves. Cultural tourism is very much a part of French education and socialization. Often a family will spend part of its vacation following the itinerary in one of the regional green Michelin guides while a designated family member reads aloud the guide's explanation of the places and buildings of historical and cultural significance. The Michelin guide is something of a cultural icon itself, and reference to it evokes in the French a vision of the bourgeois family vacation. The most popular cultural attractions for French tourists are the Louvre museum, Versailles palace, the Orsay museum of Impressionist painters in Paris, the Abbey of St. Michel in Normandy, and Chambord and Chenonceaux Castles in the Loire Valley.

The pleasure the French get from visiting cultural monuments and museums is enhanced by their knowledge of the historical events that have molded their nation and of the characteristics of the art forms in each century. The artifacts and historical events, being a shared cultural experience, serve as examples and points of reference in French conversations and form the basis for the "cultural baggage" that is an important component of being French. And the French are proud of their rich cultural heritage that has built up through the centuries since the time of the prehistoric cave drawings in the southwest region of Périgord and the Roman settlements after Julius Caesar's invasion of Gaul in 52 BC.

While visiting and admiring their cultural treasures, the French persuade themselves that their civilization is superior to all others, that France is the most civilized of all nations, and that the French way of doing things is the best conceivable way. Many foreigners share the French admiration of the masterpieces of French culture but are critical of what they see as the cultural arrogance of the French.

❁

18. CULTURE

French governments have always promoted a cultural heritage policy within France as well as actively promoting French language and culture throughout the world. The high-culture image of France is generally associated with masterpieces of architecture, painting, sculpture, and music. The Gothic cathedrals, the Impressionist painters, the sculptures by Auguste Rodin (1840–1917) and the music of Hector Berlioz (1803–69) have become icons of international cultural comparison. Examples of French painting are considered to be an essential component of the leading art museums throughout the world. Art museums in all regions of France exhibit French paintings from the various centuries. In Paris the main museums are the Louvre, which displays art works up to 1850; the Orsay Museum, which opened in 1986 and displays works from 1850 to 1914; and the Beaubourg Museum (also called the Georges Pompidou Center), which opened in 1977 for contemporary painting. Not strictly French, but worth mentioning in this context, is the Picasso Museum, which opened in Paris in 1985 to display the paintings, drawings, and sculptures of the Spanish-born Pablo Picasso (1881–1973), arguably the most influential artist of the twentieth century, who did most of his work in France, where he lived from 1904 until his death.

Literature and theater are other forms of high culture that have made France famous around the world by inspiring writers, philosophers, poets, playwrights, and theater directors in many countries.

❈

19. DECORATIONS

A small ribbon or a rosette on the left lapel of a French man's or woman's coat is a state award for outstanding civil or military service. A red ribbon or rosette denotes the highest state award, the **Légion d'honneur,** created by Napoleon Bonaparte (1769–1821) in 1802, and is accorded particular respect.

Each state honor has several grades, designated by the form of the decoration: a ribbon for **chevalier,** the lowest grade; a rosette for **officier,** the next grade; a rosette on a silver **nœud** for **commandeur,** the highest grade. Some other state honors are the **Ordre national du mérite** (blue); **Ordre des Palmes académiques** (for service to education, mauve); **Ordre des Arts et des Lettres** (for contributions to arts and literature, green). French people in these areas of endeavor greatly covet these marks of professional and social rank, which are awarded in the name of the president of the Republic.

❈

20. DOCUMENTS AND FORMS

A French citizen becomes a legal adult at the age of 18; from that age one is entitled to vote in national elections and obligated to carry at all times the national identity card **(carte nationale d'identité),** which shows the citizen's name, date of birth, physical characteristics, address, photograph (head shot), and an official stamp. Until adulthood, a child's name and date of birth is officially recorded in the **livret de famille** (family booklet).

Identity documents must be produced when requested by the police or as official papers when requested by public administration offices. Of course, for visitors, passports serve in the place of national identity cards.

Other important personal documents are the French passport (whose cover is identical throughout the European Union); the **carte de sécurité sociale,** demonstrating citizenship and therefore entitlement to national health benefits; and the **carte d'allocations familiales** (government grants are given to families with children as part of a policy to increase the national birth rate). In addition, all car drivers must have a **permis de conduire** (driver's license) and a **carte grise** with registration details of the car.

The large number and frequent use of these documents in daily life reflects the influence of the state in France. A French citizen goes to the **mairie** (city hall) and other administrative offices to keep all these documents up to date and have them stamped. The civil servants there have a fearsome reputation for applying the letter of the law strictly. The excessive bureaucratic attitudes and large number of forms to be filled out often cause French displays of frustration and annoyance and provide opportunities for the citizenry to exercise their wits in finding ways to circumvent the legal requirements.

❁

21. DRINKING

French wines and liqueurs are famous throughout the world. France is the second-largest wine producer; Italy produces more wine, but the French drink more of it. Wine is drunk in moderation with meals, and children are sometimes given a drop of wine in their glass of water on special occasions.

The most famous wine growing regions are Alsace (for white wines), Bordeaux and Burgundy (for both red and white wines), and Beaujolais (for light red wines). Champagne is produced from vineyards between Rheims and Épernay, to the east of Paris.

Most French houses and apartment buildings feature a **cave** (cellar) in which bottles of vintage wine are stored for special meals and family celebrations. Wine for daily meals **(vin de table)** can be bought from the supermarket or wine shop.

The French also drink a large quantity of mineral water **(eau minérale),** sold in bottles. The Ministry of Health must recognize genuine therapeutic qualities before it will agree to allow a water to be labeled **eau minérale. Eau** can be either **gazeuse** (bubbly; Perrier is an international example) or **plate** (still; like Evian). Both water and wine appear on the table at mealtime. French households drink more than twice as much mineral water as wine.

The drinks served at a formal meal follow a set order: an **apéritif** (cocktail), white wine with the **hors d'œuvre,** as well as with the main course if it is fish or veal, red wine with a main course of red meat or game and with the cheese, champagne with the cake or dessert if the meal is a celebration, and a liqueur or **digestif** such as cognac or a fruit liqueur after coffee.

There are two famous **apéritifs,** by the way. The first is **kir** (named after a Dijon priest who was a hero in the Resistance), made by mixing black currant liqueur **(cassis)** with white wine—or with champagne, in which case it is a **kir royal.** The second is **pastis,** the brand name of an aniseed-flavored spirit that is popular mostly in the South and mostly in the summer.

Usually only workers will drink wine together in a café. Friends from other social groups meeting for a drink will order a coffee, a beer, or fruit juice. Today Coca-Cola is making headway among French teenagers; for a long time it was unpopular because they thought it had an aftertaste of medicine.

The North and East of France, which border beer-drinking Germany, Belgium, and Holland, have a beer-drinking tradition and produce two popular brands of French beer, Kronenbourg and Kanterbrau. France in general is only the seventh-largest in beer consumption in Europe. It was a Frenchman, Louis Pasteur (1822–95), who in 1873 successfully devised a method to kill disease-producing organisms in beer by raising the temperature in the brewing process.

❁

22. DRIVING

Renault, Peugeot, and Citroën are cars of French design that are exported to many countries. They are, with Fiat and Volkswagen, the major European car manufacturers. The Renault Company, founded in 1899 by Louis Renault (1877–1944), was nationalized in 1945. More than half of French drivers own a French-made car. Import quotas limit the number of Japanese cars on French roads.

An extensive network of **autoroutes** (national superhighways) covers France. A great many are toll roads **(autoroutes à péage).** Traffic on the **autoroutes** is very heavy at the beginning and end of weekends and during the summer vacation of July and August. Drivers sometimes use the national roads to avoid paying tolls even though the French generally believe that time is more important than money.

A common French motoring expression is **conduire comme un fou** (to drive like a madman). The traffic congestion at peak times brings out the impatient, aggressive, and argumentative side of the French nature. French individualism militates against cooperation between drivers, who use their horns or, when the horn is not loud or raucous enough to do justice to their outrage, scream abuse at any driver who seems to challenge their right to proceed immediately and unimpeded to their destinations.

French drivers dislike paying in underground parking lots, and so in congested Paris they often leave their cars parked on the sidewalk or across building entrances. The Parisian driving experience provides further challenges in the trucks and cars double parked for deliveries or for shopping on the way home. Abuse of parking regulations and failure to pay parking fines is not discouraged by the genial practice of general amnesty on French parking tickets at the installation of each new president of the Republic.

France has an extremely high number of traffic accidents despite stiff speeding fines and frequent use of radar. A new system in which accumulated traffic offenses can mean the loss of one's license has not yet had an appreciable effect on the rate of accidents, but time will tell.

Huge crowds of car-racing enthusiasts are attracted to the **24 heures du Mans** (a 24-hour car race at Le Mans in the West), the Monte Carlo Rally, and the rally from Paris to Dakar (the capital of Senegal in Africa).

❁

23. ECOLOGY

France protects the flora, fauna, and ecological environment in the large state national parks, principally in the mountain regions of the Alps, the Pyrénées, the Cévennes, and in the Camargue on the Mediterranean coast. Marine life and the ecology of small islands are protected in underwater national parks around the French Mediterranean and Corsica. Jacques Cousteau (1910–), the famous underwater explorer, is a leading French environmentalist.

The Green movement did not develop a wide social base in France until the late 1980s. It grew out of the Student Revolt of May 1968 as a protest movement, but the 1974 oil crisis and the resulting economic crisis of the late 1970s and 1980s relegated the movement to a minor role in the French political dialogue. Part of the government's response to France's energy crisis and lack of oil and other natural energy resources was to develop a strong base of nuclear energy, and the strategy enjoyed wide public support, further weakening the Green movement's appeal.

Several events of the late 1980s galvanized French concern over environmental issues, and French attitudes shifted dramatically. In 1986 the Chernobyl nuclear reactor disaster threatened all Europe with nuclear fallout. French news media, like news media around the world, also focused attention on the recently discovered gap in the ozone layer, the greenhouse effect, acid rain, and the destruction of the Amazon rain forest. A number of oil tanker accidents polluted stretches of the French coastline. There are two Green political parties, **les Verts** and **Génération Écologie,** the former being the more idealistic of the two. Together they polled 14.4 percent of the votes cast in the 1992 regional elections, but at least some of that total can be attributed to public disillusionment with the traditional political parties. The degree of actual permanent commitment of French voters to ecological ideals has declined since.

❁

24. EDUCATION

French parents have a constant preoccupation with the education of their children. Children who achieve top grades in France's national educational system based on intellectual merit without concern for wealth or privilege can expect the financial and social rewards of a brilliant career. Intellectually gifted children from the French working class benefit from this democratic principle and can graduate with excellent career opportunities and the prospect of climbing the social ladder.

The primary and secondary schools are administered nationally, which means that the course content and examinations are the same for all French students. The state subsidizes private (mostly religious) schools, which make up 14 percent of the primary schools and 21 percent of the secondary schools. The subsidies are still controversial in Republican France.

French pupils become accustomed to long hours at school and lots of homework from an early age. Primary school classes start between 8 and 8:30 AM; there is a two-hour break for lunch and classes end after 4:30. Children then come home, have a snack, and do their homework, which is often supervised by their mothers, before having dinner at 7:00 PM or later.

Students in their final secondary school year (at around the age of eighteen) discuss the **baccalauréat** exam with great anxiety and anticipation. They are under pressure to receive good grades on this final exam at high school because its results determine their future study and career possibilities. A perfect score on the **bac** is 20; students who score above 10 are entitled to enroll in one of the universities, all of which are state-financed. Because of the tremendous number of students enrolled in first-year university classes, students must learn to work independently and receive far less guidance and personal assistance than American students from their instructors. Most assessment is done by formal exams requiring high intellectual performance and acting as barriers to stop a large proportion of students from progressing to their senior year.

Students with the highest grades on the **baccalauréat** may decide to enroll in a preparatory class for one of the entrance examinations to the **Grandes Écoles** instead of enrolling in a normal university. There are about a hundred **Grandes Écoles,** also state-financed, whose purpose is to prepare students for certain elite professions. Only the best students pass the barrier of the competitive entrance examinations to these **Écoles,** whose diplomas in many cases are a virtual guarantee of a high-ranking position in a particular profession. In such a hierarchical system, parents' obsession with their children's scholastic performance in primary and secondary school is understandable.

If the students at a **Grande École** are the crème de la crème of higher-education students, what more can be said about those who enter the highest-ranking of the **Grandes Écoles?** Graduates of the **École polytechnique,** originally founded by Napoleon (1769–1821) in 1804 as a military school, dominate private industry, while graduates of the **École Nationale d'Administration** (they are called **énarques**), a school established by Charles de Gaulle (1890–1970) in 1945 to train government administrators, have a virtual monopoly on all significant government positions. Many presidents and prime ministers have been **énarques,** including Valéry Giscard d'Estaing (1926–   ), Jacques Chirac (1932–   ), Laurent Fabius (1946–   ), Michel Rocard (1930–   ), and Édouard Balladur (1929–   ).

All attempts to reform this rigid educational system provoke heated controversy among parents who want their children to benefit from its hierarchical structure, and from secondary and university students, who are quick to organize street demonstrations.

❁

25. EUROPE

Two Frenchmen, Robert Schuman (1886–1963) and Jean Monnet (1888–1979) are called the founders of modern Europe. Schumann proposed the European Coal and Steel Community (the first United Europe project, ratified in 1951). Despite their traditional rivalry, France and Germany have taken the initiative in constructing the European Union. The European Union has added some terms of Euro-jargon to French vocabulary: **Eurocrate, Europhile, Eurosceptique, Eurocentrique,** and **Europol** (the police force). Will this Euro-vocabulary gain *de jure* acceptance by the **Académie française?**

Six countries (Belgium, France, Germany, Italy, Luxembourg, and The Netherlands) signed the Rome Treaty in 1957 to create the European Economic Community (EEC, popularly called the Common Market). Denmark, Ireland, and the United Kingdom applied to join them and were admitted in 1973; Greece joined in 1981 and Spain and Portugal in 1986. In 1992 these twelve signed the Maastricht Treaty and established the European Union, an entity with 345 million inhabitants and no trade barriers between member countries—a powerful economic bloc comparable to the United States and Japan. Austria, Finland, Sweden, and Norway have been accepted as members of the European Union as of 1995.

The European Union will develop the present internal trade and labor agreements into a more unified common economic and monetary policy, and eventually closer political ties, although there are large obstacles to the last goal, as one might imagine. Members had conflicting reactions to the invasion of Kuwait by Iraq in 1992 and to the wars between the republics of the former Yugoslavia that began in 1993. The Union did, however, show a capacity for united action during the 1993 GATT treaty negotiations, when France led the way to important cultural concessions for Europe in the final treaty.

The European Commission, located in Brussels, Belgium, administers the Union. A Frenchman, Jacques Delors (1925–   ), presided over it from 1985 to 1995. The European Parliament is located in Strasbourg, France, where it meets monthly. Extraordinary sessions and meetings of its committees take place in Brussels. Its members are elected for five-year terms in national elections; its first president was a Frenchwoman, Simone Veil (1927–   ). Seats are apportioned by population. In the 567-seat legislature elected in 1994, Germany was allotted 99 seats, France, Italy, and Britain 87 each, Spain 64, The Netherlands 31, Belgium, Greece, and Portugal 25 each, Denmark 16, Ireland 15, and Luxembourg 7.

The Parliament's powers were mostly advisory until the Maastricht Treaty gave it power to approve the European Commission's budget and amend its decisions, block agreements with outside countries, and veto appointments to the European Union executive agencies. These changes were aimed at giving the elected body representing the European citizens more control over the European Commission bureaucracy and involving them more closely in the functioning of European democracy and the formulation of European Union policy. In bringing together the elected representatives of twelve countries who debate in nine languages and vote democratically on all legislation, the 1994 European Parliament is a unique institution in the world.

When France held a national referendum in 1992 to ratify the signing of the Maastricht Treaty, a deep division arose between those who supported closer integration of member countries and those who, fearing a loss of French identity in a Europe that was *too* unified, wanted a more independent France within Europe. The latter position was also that of Charles de Gaulle (1890–1970), who, while he was president from 1958 to 1969, wanted only a loose association of independent nations and opposed any suggestion of a supranational entity or identity. French presidents since 1969 have in general been more in favor. of European integration. President François Mitterrand's (1916–   ) personal campaign in favor of ratifying the Maastricht Treaty helped achieve the narrow margin of approval for it in the French referendum that took France into the European Union.

The French economy is almost certain to become increasingly integrated with that of the rest of Europe. The French, who already carry the uniform European passports, will find their lives increasingly influenced by the decisions of the new European institutions. At the same time, other Europeans will find their lives influenced by France, which constitutes 23 percent of the Union's land area and 16.5 percent of its population.

❌

26. *EXTRA!*

English and French both borrowed the Latin word *extra*. Like many French words that resemble English words, the French meaning is different. A French teenager who says **"Cette glace est extra!"** does not mean that it costs more, but that it is fantastic. **Extra** in French is a colloquial shortening of **extraordinaire,** "extraordinary."

Some other false friends of English speakers in French are **le foot,** "soccer"; **le car,** "bus (the touring kind)"; and **la location,** "hiring" or "renting." The real words for *foot, car,* and *location* are, of course, **le pied, la voiture,** and **l'endroit.**

❌

27. FAMILY

The family unit is extremely important at all levels of French society. Attitudes toward marriage and divorce have changed significantly in recent years, but the family remains the nucleus of daily and social life. In a 1991 survey, 81 percent of respondents said that the family must remain the basic unit of society and 69 percent said the family is the only place where one feels comfortable and relaxed.

Families with a large number of children have become the exception. The average number of children is 1.6 and this is barely sufficient to maintain the present population. The government gives generous family allowances to encourage couples to have more children. In families where at least one parent is a foreigner, the average number of children is higher, and 15 percent of all French births are in such families. Unmarried parents produce 30 percent of France's babies.

Mealtimes play an essential role in maintaining the nuclear family unit. Children are expected to sit at the table and have their meals with their parents. This is one of the many forms of disciplined socialization that results in French children who behave like adults from an early age and who have a strong sense of belonging to a family. The extended family gathers on many occasions to celebrate family events with a special meal. The extended network of relations provides valuable social and career support as the children move through adolescence and begin to enter the work force.

Moral and financial support from the family has assumed even more importance during the past decade of economic crises. At sixteen, 95 percent of French children live with their parents; at twenty, 60 percent of males and 45 percent of females do. When children do leave home, they tend to live fairly close to their parents and vacations usually include time with the extended family.

❁

28. FASHION

Each year in January and August, when Paris's leading fashion designers present their new collections, the city reasserts its position as

29

the fashion capital of the world. The influence becomes obvious as the season's styles in other countries begin to appear.

The founder of modern fashion was Charles Worth (1825–95), an Englishman who settled in Paris in 1845 and established the first **maison de haute couture** there in 1858. His dress designs, using the highest-quality workmanship and materials, dictated women's fashions at the court of Emperor Napoleon III (1808–73), and the other courts of Europe imitated them. Worth also dressed the richest women on other continents.

The international supremacy of French fashion was facilitated by the invention of the Singer sewing machine, which increased productivity of the fashion houses. Until the 1850s **haute couture** dresses were completely handmade, and handwork remained their distinguishing feature, but seamstresses using the Singer could produce the basic stitching more quickly.

The work of Paul Poiret (1879–1944) and Coco Chanel (1883–1971) set the fashion for a more fluid, comfortable style, freeing women from their corsets. Chanel pioneered the use of jersey, a supple fabric, and the wearing of costume jewelry.

Paris's reputation was enhanced when leading designers opened numerous **haute couture** houses there: Jean Patou (1880–1936), Madeleine Vionnet (1876–1975), and Jeanne Lanvin (1867–1946).

Christian Dior (1905–57) launched the New Look in 1947 after years of austerity and deprivation during the Second World War and reestablished Paris as the trend setter. Pierre Cardin (1922–   ) and Yves Saint-Laurent (1936–   ) continued Dior's success; their new fashion silhouettes were copied worldwide. More recently Jean-Paul Gaultier (1952–   ) has made an impact and was chosen by Madonna to design her stage costumes. Designers also market their own labels of prestige perfumes that have become as famous as their fashions.

All contemporary designers create ready-to-wear clothes and accessories as well as exclusive **haute couture** gowns, a nod to the changing lifestyles and budgets of modern career women. Despite the new generation of women whose values have been influenced by feminism, French fashion trends continue to be an object of interest, fascination, and fantasy for the huge readership of women's magazines across the world.

29. FLOWERS AND GARDENS

Red roses are a symbol of love and beauty in France, as in many countries. Chrysanthemums, however, have a special meaning; you don't give them to your loved ones unless they are dead. The French traditionally place chrysanthemums on family graves in visits on **Toussaint** (All Saint's Day) on November 1. A flower is also associated with the Labor Day holiday **(Fête du Travail);** the lily-of-the-valley **(muguet)** is given to friends and family on that day to bring them happiness **(un porte-bonheur).**

The French style of garden **(jardin à la française)** is geometrical, with frequent use of ponds, fountains, and statues; the landscape architect André Le Nôtre (1613–1700), who designed the gardens of the Versailles Palace, originated it. The Tuileries Gardens near the Louvre and the Luxembourg Gardens near the Sorbonne, both in Paris, are examples of the style. The Impressionist painter Claude Monet's (1840–1926) garden at Giverny in Normandy, where he painted his radiant ''Water Lilies'' **(''Nymphéas'')** series from 1899 to his death, and which has been maintained with the help of American philanthropists, also attracts crowds of admiring visitors.

❁

30. FRIENDSHIP

The French make a clear distinction between friends **(amis, amies)** and acquaintances **(connaissances).** Foreigners have often observed that it is not easy to progress beyond acquaintance and become accepted as a friend in France. A casual relationship develops into friendship only after a considerable amount of time. The French usually have only a small number of close friends **(grand[e]s ami[e]s)** in addition to their immediate family. Friends expect loyalty and sincerity from each other, tend to belong to the same social background, and remain true friends throughout their lives.

Patterns of friendship are changing as today's young generation travels more, becomes more outward-looking, and adopts a more relaxed approach to life. Students use the **tu** form automatically with each other instead of the **vous** form, which is traditionally used when people meet for the first time. Shared interests and intellectual affinities are increasingly the reason for becoming friends. Such friendships cut across social barriers, which previously limited the possibilities of making close friends outside one's social group.

❈

31. FROGS AND SNAILS, GARLIC AND TRUFFLES

An old British cliché parodies the French as a bizarre people who constantly eat frogs, snails, garlic, and tree-root fungi such as truffles—a disgusting diet to the British palate accustomed to its healthful and eye-appealing diet of greasy fried potatoes and greasier fried fish. The cliché gave rise to the popular British name for the French, the "Frogs."

This national cliché is as exaggerated as all national clichés are. These food items are relatively uncommon on French menus, with the exception of garlic, which figures in many dishes as it does in all Mediterranean cuisines. Some restaurants offer frogs' legs and Burgundy snails as appetizers before the main course. Pigs are trained to find black truffles, a rare and expensive delicacy that grows symbiotically on hazelnut roots in the South of France. The French Christmas meal traditionally features a tiny bit of truffle on another delicacy, **foie gras** (the liver of geese that have been force-fed to enlarge their livers), accompanied by champagne.

So much of French life involves eating and culinary traditions that English-influenced countries which give little importance to fine food satirize the French as obsessive about their stomachs and make fun of what they select from nature to put on their plates.

❈

32. GAMBLING

Napoleon Bonaparte (1769–1821) outlawed gambling for money, and it has been illegal continuously since—except, of course, for state-run gambling activities, whose revenues account for a great deal of government income. More than 50 percent of the French population participates hoping that their luck will win them some money.

Most such state income flows from the PMU **(Pari mutuel urbain),** which controls off-course betting on horse racing. Bettors line up in cafés on Sundays to bet on **le tiercé** (choosing first through third place correctly), **le quarté** (choosing first through fourth place correctly), or **le quinté** (choosing first through fifth place correctly). Eighty percent of PMU gamblers are men and by far the largest proportion of them come from the working classes.

Loto has superseded the National Lottery and attracts more gamblers than the PMU but brings in less state revenue. Scratch lottery tickets (like instant lotteries) such as **Cash, Surf,** and **Banco** are growing in popularity, but the favorite among the French is **le Millionaire,** which includes the extra chance of adding to one's winnings on a television show. French television, in fact, has many game shows that attract a large audience.

The state also runs gambling casinos, but they are few and are patronized largely by the upper class. They contribute only a small percentage of the state's overall income from gambling.

❁

33. GASTRONOMY AND RESTAURANTS

French cuisine is famous around the world and the French themselves are famous for their enjoyment of fine food. A constant reason that tourists give for visiting France is to eat French food and go to a French restaurant. The authoritative Michelin guide classifies top French restaurants as three-, two-, and one-star. A chef at a restaurant that achieves three stars becomes internationally famous by that very fact.

The high standards of French chefs did not begin in this century. Vatel, the principal chef of the Prince de Condé (1621–86), killed himself with his own sword in 1671 because the seafood had not arrived in time for a dinner the prince was giving in honor of King Louis XIV (1638–1715). The story goes that it was Marie de Médicis (1573–1642)—and the Italian chefs she brought to France with her as a safeguard against the uncertain quality of food preparation in her adopted country—who began the French tradition of fine cooking.

French culinary traditions have been popularized internationally by famous chefs such as Marie-Antoine Carême (1784–1833);
Auguste Escoffier (1846–1935), whose *Guide Culinaire* (1920) is still
used today by cooks in every country; and Paul Bocuse (1926–   ),
whose international television programs have added a new dimension
to the French bourgeois style of cooking by the use of fresh seasonal
market produce.

In the 1980s chef Michel Olivier (1932–   ) introduced a new
style of cooking called **nouvelle cuisine** or **cuisine minceur** (thin
cooking), which spread to fine restaurants everywhere and influenced
new California cuisine. **Nouvelle cuisine** eliminated excessive butter
and fats from traditional French sauces and recipes and highlighted
the artistic presentation of small portions of food on the diner's plate.

Some leading chefs of today, such as Joël Robuchon (1945–   ),
are directing their creative talents to simple family recipes their
grandmothers used and to combinations of Asian and French flavors.
The recipes of many countries use French cooking expressions (**sauté,
roux, lardon**), and French dishes appear on restaurant menus in
many countries.

France is an agriculturally rich country and the diversity of market produce in its regions has created lasting regional food traditions.
Choucroute garnie in Alsace, **cassoulet** in the Southwest, **bouillabaisse** along the Mediterranean coast, and **couscous** from Algeria
and other former North African colonies are well known among
them. Towns and provinces have become bywords by virtue of their
best-known food products and found permanent places in French gastronomic tradition: Dijon mustard, the Champagne province's spar-
kling wine, Bordeaux red wines, the brandy of Cognac, Bresse
chicken, and Roquefort cheese are only a few examples. The hum-
blest staple food has so many entrenched regional variations that
Charles de Gaulle (1890–1970) could invoke the diversity as a symbol
of the characteristic French individualism: **"Un pays qui compte
350 sortes de fromage, c'est ingouvernable"** (A country with 350
kinds of cheese is ungovernable).

The number of American-inspired fast-food restaurants has increased in France, as have the sales of frozen foods. The modern
working woman has less time these days for elaborate recipes. All the
same, the French cook still seeks out the best suppliers of fresh pro-

duce in the markets and the French list eating as their principal source of pleasure. The seasonal arrival of asparagus and strawberries is a gastronomic event that occasions celebration and conversation at the family dining table.

The French playwright Molière (1622–73) wrote **"Il faut manger pour vivre et ne pas vivre pour manger"** (You must eat to live and not live to eat). Possibly Marie de Médicis had not yet achieved her gastronomic revolution in France by the time he wrote that, but whatever the case, French people today typically paraphrase his words in reverse, to express personal and national satisfaction in the delights of their tables. The festive atmosphere produced by delicious food, wine, and animated conversation expresses the conviviality for which the French are justly famous. As the gastronome Brillat Savarin (1755–1826) wrote, **"Un bon repas favorise la conversation; un bon vin lui donne de l'esprit"** (A good meal encourages conversation; a good wine makes it spirited).

❁

34. GENDARMES AND DEMONSTRATIONS

The police officers charged with traffic control and security outside cities are called **gendarmes,** based at the local **gendarmerie.** In cities they are **agents de police,** based at the local **commissariat de police** (police station). Their mission is the usual range of law and order enforcement and traffic control, and they also play a major role in the administrative supervision of foreign and immigrant residents.

France has a history of large politically motivated street demonstrations (**manifestations,** or **manifs**), in which people of all ages and from all walks of life take part if they feel strongly on the subject. Van loads of police parked on side streets supervise peaceful **manifs** vigilantly, and the CRS (**Compagnies Républicaines de Sécurité,** the riot police) will be on hand if passions seem likely to run high—as they typically do on issues of school and university reform, agricultural grievances caused by European Union policies, or race relations.

The police are authorized to conduct random identity checks (**contrôle d'identité**) by asking for the national identity card in the street or in metro or train stations. The police usually concentrate such efforts on people of African or North African appearance because of concern with illegal immigration.

❀

35. GESTURES

Italians are often parodied for their dramatic gestures when they speak. The French, especially southerners, also gesture a lot. Even naturally undemonstrative French people draw from a large stock of facial expressions and bodily gestures to add force or nuance to the spoken word.

Americans are socially trained to smile a lot; the French are not. In fact, when asked for an opinion, their first reaction is to pout with the lips. Foreigners who are not used to this reaction may incorrectly interpret this frequent French pouting as a sign of their rudeness or contempt for people from other countries.

Almost no gesture is universal, but some gestures are at least multinational. The American gesture for "Crazy," circling the index finger near the temple, closely resembles the French gesture with the same meaning, pointing the index finger at the temple and twisting the hand back and forth. The English expression "My foot!" translates into French as **Mon œil!** (my eye), and the French expression has a convenient gesture that can accompany or replace it: pulling the lower eyelid down slightly with the index finger. This gesture is also a convenient and quick way of indicating to the other listeners that you don't believe the speaker's version of events.

Several parts of the body may coordinate in French gestures. To say "I don't know" or "Beats me" **(J' sais pas),** a French person can pout lips, raise eyebrows, push his or her head forward slightly, raise shoulders, and raise the hands to shoulder level with palms out and upward.

French start counting from the thumb, not the index finger. An American ordering two beers in France with the index and middle finger might well receive three, however energetically the American's thumb was curled out of sight.

French tend to stand or lean closer to each other in conversation than Americans do. Two French speakers standing close, leaning toward each other, and employing the standard set of gestures gives an American observer the impression that the two are speaking intensely and reacting with animated emotion. It is wise to remember that this is style and habit and not to be misled into drawing psychological conclusions about the speakers or the national temperament from such observations. The two could be total strangers, one of whom asked the other for the time of day.

❂

36. GOVERNMENT AND POLITICS

France is a republic, and the majority of French people take pride in their country's history and place in the world. Since the Declaration of the Rights of Man and of the Citizen in 1789, **la République** has known many ups and downs. France is currently in its Fifth Republic, which was founded by Charles de Gaulle (1890–1970) in 1958. It is a presidential regime in which voters elect their president for a seven-year term in a national direct vote, elect a National Assembly for five-year terms, and vote at other times for councils of their **région** and locality and for French representatives in the European Parliament.

From 1981 to 1995 the French president was François Mitterrand (1916–   ), a politician and elder statesman of consummate skill. Not the least of his achievements was to have been elected as a socialist and reelected in 1988 for a total of fourteen years while governments of the left and right came and went during his tenure. As head of state, the president has considerable powers but is expected to leave the day-to-day running of the country to the prime minister and his or her government.

The prime minister is selected from the majority party in the National Assembly by the president. The prime minister then appoints a government (a set of ministers) with the president's approval and runs the country according to the Assembly majority's political program. The members of the government don't have to be elected members of the National Assembly or even belong to the prime minister's party. When the president and the prime minister are from different political parties, they must agree to cooperate according to the functions of their office as defined in the Constitution. This arrangement is called **cohabitation.**

Local politics remain extremely important in France. Councilors **(conseillers)** elected by the residents of regions, departments, and communes hold power under the reform legislation of the 1980s decentralizing administration in France. The smallest administrative unit is the commune, of which there are 36,000 in France. Each commune has a mayor, elected by the members of the municipal council.

The French have traditionally been a very political people, with active left-wing (socialist and communist) organizations, powerful conservative parties, and other small parties such as the extreme right and the Greens. The political passions engaged in ideological conflicts often lead to street demonstrations against government decisions. The left had a decade of power in the 1980s that included France's first woman prime minister, Édith Cresson (1934–   ), but the left's power dissipated in the country's recession and chronic unemployment and internal party ills. A pragmatic conservative government under prime minister Édouard Balladur (1929–   ) replaced the socialist government in 1993.

37. *GRANDEUR*

Grandeur was the heart of the concept of France that General Charles de Gaulle (1890–1970) developed to restore the self-confidence and pride of a nation that had capitulated to the German army and accepted Nazi occupation from 1940 to 1944. The Vichy régime (officially **l'État Français**) under Marshal Philippe Pétain (1856–1951) collaborated with Hitler during that time and carried out Hitler's policies in France, while General de Gaulle commanded the Free French Forces and the French Resistance from exile. Although de Gaulle's army played a relatively small role in the Allied liberation of Europe and Pétain's collaboration weakened France's moral position in the armistice, de Gaulle insisted that France occupy an equal footing with the Soviet Union, the United Kingdom, and the United States at the Yalta Conference at the end of the Second World War. De Gaulle identified **grandeur** with France's position as an independent nation of the world.

During de Gaulle's presidency of the Fifth Republic from 1958 to 1969, his determination to have France play a leading role in world affairs independent of the two superpowers that emerged from Yalta, the United States and the Soviet Union, guided his foreign policy. He became the self-proclaimed voice of the developing countries who were struggling to gain independence, and he criticized American involvement in Vietnam. His repeated affirmation of France's **grandeur** and democratic principles and his frequent opposition to "Anglo-Saxon" (American and British) foreign policy gave the French at home pride in their country's stature and achievements, while for their part the "Anglo-Saxons" were often irritated by his claims and behavior, which they regarded as unjustified and extremely arrogant. The conservative Gaullist party that traces its ideological heritage to General de Gaulle still plays a major role in French government.

De Gaulle's foreign policy added arrogance to the foreign image of the French themselves, and that image has resurfaced every time a French president, however pro-American the regime in question, has taken an independent view in world affairs.

❁

38. GREETINGS AND FAREWELLS

The formal etiquette of shaking hands or kissing family members on both cheeks **(la bise)** when meeting or saying goodbye remains a core tradition that all French people observe. Even friends who use the informal **Salut!** as the accompanying greeting or farewell will shake hands or offer **la bise.**

When people are meeting for the first time or when they are of unequal social or professional status, the handshake is always used and the verbal greeting takes the form of **Bonjour, Madame** (or **Monsieur** or **Mademoiselle**), without the person's name. The formal farewell is **Au revoir, (Madame/Monsieur/Mademoiselle).** To address casually a mixture of men and women, the French may shorten the term of address to **Messieurs-Dames,** as in **Au revoir, Messieurs-Dames.**

The initial greeting is followed by a *de rigueur* question about the person's morale or health. Informally, the question is usually **Ça va?** Otherwise, a choice must be made between the formal **vous** and the friendly **tu: Vous allez bien?** or **Tu vas bien?** Foreigners in doubt should use the **vous** form and pay attention to whether their French acquaintance indicates the relationship has become informal or close enough to be at the **tu** stage—except in the case of student with student, which is invariably **tu** unless a speaker wants to signal a special reason for distance.

A person leaving a group in France will often take leave with **Au revoir, tout le monde!** (Goodbye, everyone.) Sometimes one in the group will indulge in a joke that has by now become stale and reply, **Au revoir, tout(e) seul(e)!** (Goodbye, all alone.) A foreigner who uses this joke might receive one of three reactions: dismay that an embarrassing trivium of modern French life has become common knowledge in the outside world, delight to hear an old favorite from unexpected lips, or the obligatory groans. Receiving the last would probably be a sign of acceptance as an equal.

The greeting and farewell expressions in professional and personal letters are strictly codified in their levels of formality, which takes some getting used to. The most formal level, again, omits first and family names and begins with a bare **Monsieur, Madame,** or **Mademoiselle.** The addition of **Cher (Chère)** colors the formality with a shade of warmth. The first name is used in letters between family members and close friends: **Mon cher Pierre, Ma chère Isabelle.**

Farewell expressions in French letters strike English speakers as particularly wordy, complex, and flowery. One or another variation of the terse Anglo-Saxon ''Yours sincerely'' appears in the most hastily scrawled letters. The form of address that appeared in the opening greeting reappears in the farewell at the end. Some examples from very formal to relatively informal are

> **Veuillez agreer, Monsieur, l'expression de mes sentiments les plus distingués** (Please be willing to accept, Sir, the expression of my most distinguished sentiments)

> **Je vous prie de recevoir, cher Monsieur, l'expression de mes salutations les meilleures** (I beg you to accept, dear Sir, the expression of my best greetings)

Je t'envoie, ma chère Isabelle, mon amical souvenir (I send you, my dear Isabelle, my friendly remembrance)

Adept French letter writers will construct many variations to express the relationship precisely, but these three models will serve English speakers who have not worked with the forms from early childhood. The first is appropriate for most business letters to customers or suppliers or when applying for information, the second to colleagues or acquaintances, the third for close friendships that are well established. When in doubt between two choices, opt for the more formal of the two and observe the form that appears in the reply.

❁

39. GUILLOTINE

A professor of anatomy, Joseph Guillotin (1738–1814), invented a machine and proposed in 1789 that it be used to cut off the heads of the people that Revolutionary organizations condemned to death. The most famous victims of the guillotine were King Louis XVI (1754–93) and Queen Marie-Antoinette (1755–93), who were beheaded in public in 1793 on the square now called **Place de la Concorde** in Paris.

France continued to use the guillotine to execute criminals whom the courts condemned to death until the government of Socialist president François Mitterrand (1916–   ) abolished capital punishment in 1981.

❁

40. HEALTH AND FITNESS

The French set great store by their health **(santé),** a fact that is not surprising in a nation that produced Louis Pasteur (1822–95), the prime discoverer of microbiology; the international humanitarian group of doctors **Médecins sans Frontières** (Doctors without Borders); and the research team at the **Institut Pasteur** under Luc Montagnier (1932–   ) who were the first to discover the AIDS virus. France spends more money on health than any of its European part-

41

ners. The French love to visit their doctors and expect a high level of service when they do, involving numerous prescriptions, X rays, and hospital examinations. The French national health system, part of the social security system, was one of the earliest (1945) in Europe and reimburses every citizen's medical and hospital expenses.

The French are renowned for their enjoyment of drinking and smoking and suffer the illnesses that these pleasures entail. (Drinking is decreasing, and the government launched an antismoking campaign in 1992.) The French diet, on the other hand, consists of well-balanced meals eaten at home and moderate sweets. For all the attention that the French demand of their doctors, they often prefer home remedies and consume herbal teas for stress or insomnia and homeopathic treatment for various ailments. Many also believe in taking the cure at a spa such as Vichy. Mineral water named for a spa is popular as a remedy for various minor ills.

Possibly from a growing consciousness of sedentary habits such as watching television and sitting in cafés, possibly as a reaction to increased stress in modern French life, jogging and aerobics have become popular since the 1980s. The French have always enjoyed the less glamorous, more rural counterparts, country walking and cycling, as traditional outdoor activities.

✿

41. HEROES AND HEROINES

The French refer to their past much more and plan their future much less than Americans. Certain men and women have become legendary in French history for their exploits, and they often serve as examples, symbols, and proverbs in discussions and in news presentations.

Two examples of patriotism are Vercingetorix and Joan of Arc. Vercingetorix (72–46 BC) led the Gauls against the invading army of Julius Caesar, was defeated at Alésia in 52 BC, and surrendered valiantly. Joan of Arc (**Jeanne d'Arc,** 1412–31) was inspired by saints' voices to lead a mission to drive the English out of France, rally the dispirited French forces, and in turn inspire the passive Charles VII (1403–61) to assert his kingship and triumph over the English, ending the Hundred Years' War.

King Louis XIV (1638–1715), the Sun King **(le Roi Soleil)**, and Napoleon Bonaparte (1769–1821) are emblematic of French **grandeur** for expanding the role of France in Europe through a series of triumphs over competing nations. (The defeat of Napoleon by the English did not mitigate his lasting accomplishments as much as George IV and Wellington might have wished.) They bequeathed to French heritage, respectively, the Palace of Versailles and the Napoleonic legal code.

The French hero of the American Revolution, the Marquis de La Fayette (1757–1834), who sent President George Washington the key to the captured French Bastille from ''a missionary of Liberty to its Patriarch,'' played a significant role in the French Revolution but is better known in the United States than in France.

The engineer Gustave Eiffel (1832–1923) designed the tower that bears his name for the World Exhibition of 1889. The Eiffel Tower **(la Tour Eiffel)** has come to be a symbol of Paris.

Cyrano de Bergerac, the main character in the famous play (1897) of the same name by Edmond Rostand (1868–1918), represents the French ideal of overcoming adversity with daring and panache, not to mention wit.

The Polish-born Marie Sklodowska Curie (1867–1934) with her physicist husband Pierre (1859–1906) discovered radium. She won the Nobel Prize jointly with Pierre and Henri Becquerel in 1903 and alone in 1911. She was the first woman member of the **Académie de Médecine.**

Charles de Gaulle (1890–1970) fled to London after the German invasion in 1940 and organized the Free French Movement, which supported the Resistance against the Nazis in France. He led the liberation of Paris in 1944.

The visitor to France may occasionally hear reference to Marianne, the name the French have bestowed on the female emblem of Liberty and France herself. French actresses Brigitte Bardot (1934–   ), Catherine Deneuve (1943–   ), and Sophie Marceau (1966–   ) have served as models for the plaster sculpture of Marianne, wearing a Revolutionary bonnet, which is found inside every city hall in France.

❁

42. HEXAGON

The French often refer to their country as the Hexagon (l'Hexagone) because France has a roughly six-sided shape. Hexagonal behavior or attitudes are those that look inward nationalistically and exclude foreign points of view and influences.

❈

43. HIGH TECH

Recent French governments have assertively supported a high-tech image of France as a modern country. France is, in fact, the fourth-largest economy (after the United States, Japan, and Germany), the fourth-largest exporter, and the third-largest investor in the world. It is also the second-largest exporter of services, after the United States. Biotechnology is a fast-growing export market for France. French nuclear technology supplies three-fourths of the country's electric power. France is a major partner in the European scientific and advanced technology initiative called Eureka.

The French themselves have always been fascinated by technical inventions and have adapted quickly to new electronic and computerized aids in both their homes and businesses. The Minitel, a French-invented home computer service linked through telephone lines, was introduced in 1983 and can be found in more than 25 percent of French homes today. It also serves a large number of administrative and commercial offices and offers satellite hookups abroad. Some French and German classrooms in the United States have subscribed in order to carry on a correspondence with English classrooms in Europe.

France has a majority share in the European Space Consortium, which launches communication satellites, and the Spot land-observation satellites, from the space center in French Guiana (La Guyane). The first Ariane rocket was launched from there in 1979. The fiftieth Ariane launch occurred in 1992.

Elaborate home appliances, computerized ticket-vending machines, telephone cards, commercial laser lighting effects, the TGV (high-speed train), the VAL (driverless metro train), the Airbus air-

The Regions of France

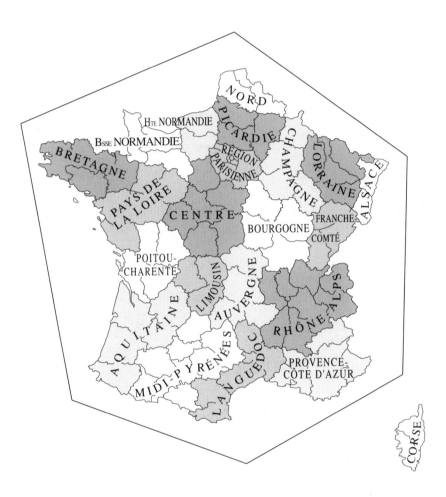

NORD

HTE NORMANDIE

PICARDIE

BSSE NORMANDIE

BRETAGNE

CHAMPAGNE

LORRAINE

RÉGION PARISIENNE

ALSACE

PAYS DE LA LOIRE

CENTRE

FRANCHE-COMTÉ

BOURGOGNE

POITOU-CHARENTE

LIMOUSIN

AUVERGNE

RHÔNE-ALPS

AQUITAINE

MIDI-PYRÉNÉES

LANGUEDOC

PROVENCE-CÔTE D'AZUR

CORSE

plane, and advanced telecommunication equipment are becoming commonplaces. A Parisian, Roland Moreno (1945–   ), invented the "smart card," which is equipped with a microchip to debit charges from the customer's bank or credit account at the point of purchase. Daily life in France is being transformed by technology.

❇

44. HOLIDAYS

All countries have their particular holidays, usually inspired by a mixture of history, religion, and paganism, and France is no exception. What is noticeable in France's case is the richness and variety of its **fêtes** (festivals): the way they point to its Catholic heritage; the French love of food and their rural past; the Revolutionary tradition.

Some traditional observances are not linked to public holidays **(jours fériés):**

Epiphany | **L'Epiphanie** (January 6). The French celebrate the Three Kings by buying a special cake, **la galette des rois,** sold for several weeks around the holiday at bakers' shops and supermarkets. The **galette** comes with a gold paper crown and conceals a tiny ceramic figure, **la fève** (bean, which it originally was). The cake is solemnly cut for dessert, and the person whose slice contains **la fève** is crowned king or queen and chooses a royal partner.

Carnival | **Le Carnaval.** Between the Epiphany and Mardi Gras (the last day before Lent, usually late February), many regions hold carnivals, which feature costumed processions and masked parades. Nice holds the biggest carnival.

La Chandeleur | (February 2). On this feast of the Virgin, it is traditional to eat pancakes **(crêpes)** at home.

April Fools | (April 1). On this day many French people indulge their mischievous practical sense of humor. Children cut out paper fish **(poissons d'avril)** and attach them to people's backs. When the fish or one of the other practical pranks of the day is revealed, the traditional cry is **Poisson d'avril!**

Mother's Day,
Father's Day   **La fête des mères** is celebrated on a Sunday in May and **la fête des pères** on a Sunday in June. The occasion is celebrated with gifts and family get-togethers. Mother's Day is the more widely observed.

Les jours fériés, official state holidays, have a civil or religious inspiration:

New Year's   **La Saint-Sylvestre** (December 31) and **le Jour de l'An** (January 1). New Year's Eve is the occasion for parties and late-night feasting **(le réveillon)** with friends and family. At midnight celebrating drivers herald the new year with a cacophony of car horns.

Easter   **Pâques.** Shops sell items that commemorate the holiday's Christian origin as well as pagan symbols of fertility—chocolate bells, fish, rabbits, and eggs.

Labor Day   **La Fête du Travail** (May 1). The holiday was instituted in France in 1947. Large trade union marches fill the streets, and many people buy sprigs of lily-of-the-valley **(muguet)** to offer friends and family with a wish for happiness.

Ascension   **L'Ascension** (Forty days after Easter, usually in May).

Pentecost   **La Pentecôte** (Fifty days after Easter). Being a Sunday, the Monday following is set aside as the day off from work and school.

National Day   **La fête nationale, le Quatorze Juillet** (July 14). This anniversary of the taking of the Bastille in 1789 strikes a chord in every French heart and is the occasion of patriotic processions, fireworks, open-air balls, and celebrations.

Assumption   **l'Assomption** (August 15). The taking of Mary into heaven has been forgotten by many French people and they treat this holiday as a bonus day attached to the beginning or end of the traditional August vaca-

| | tion. For this reason the **autoroutes** are doubly crowded with vacationers on this day with those taking off for vacation spots or returning from them. |

All Saints   **La Toussaint** (November 1). The French commemorate their dead, particularly family members, on this day by making a long journey to the family cemetery and placing chrysanthemums on the graves. The length of the journey embodies two facts of French life: the physical rift between generations, for many have moved away from their family's place of origin, and the felt need to return to a rural past and family roots.

Armistice Day   **L'Armistice** (November 11). This day marks the date of the armistice of World War I, but the end of World War II (which actually occurred on May 8, 1945) is also remembered on this day.

Christmas   **Noël** (December 25). This holiday is very much a family holiday. On Christmas Eve religiously inclined people attend midnight Mass and the whole family stays up late for **le réveillon,** a lavish traditional meal for which no expense is spared. Traditional foods are **pâté de foie gras,** oysters, turkey, and **la bûche de Noël** (a chocolate-coated cake in the form of a log), the last accompanied by a bottle of champagne. Churches display Nativity crib scenes, and in the South live lambs are placed near the cribs during midnight Mass. Children leave out shoes rather than stockings to receive the gifts from **le Père Noël** (Father Christmas).

❧

45. HOUSING

Most of the inhabitants of French cities live in apartment buildings, but the population explosion led by the post–World War II baby-boomers has caused a rapid expansion of the suburbs around the cities and, somewhat illogically, a sudden increase in the construction of individual houses. Today 58 percent of homes in France are houses rather than apartments.

The concierge, guardian of the entrance to the apartment building and traditional institution of French life, is disappearing. Modern buildings have replaced the concierge with **le gardien** or **la gardienne** or else no one at all is performing surveillance and mail distribution duties. The mail carrier **(le facteur)** puts the mail in personal letter boxes at the entrance to the building and visitors gain entrance through an intercom. To increase security against the recent rise in housebreakings and robberies, many buildings have installed a number-code lock on the street entrance door. This **code de la porte** is changed monthly or after longer intervals, and residents and visitors must know the code in order to enter.

The state had to construct cheap high-rise housing condominiums **(habitations à loyer modéré, HLM)** after 1948. Today more than 3 million families live in these unattractive tower blocks built on the periphery of cities and towns. Many of the inhabitants are immigrant and working-class families with a large number of children.

France holds the current world record for the percentage of families who own a holiday home **(une résidence secondaire)**—13 percent. Most of these families belong to the upper class, live in a city, and use the home for weekends and vacations. The demand has been met by a great many country houses that have gone up for sale as much of France's previously large rural population has migrated to the city.

The economic recession of the 1980s and its resulting unemployment created a phenomenon to which France had been unaccustomed: the homeless **(SDF: sans domicile fixe)**. Paris had always had a few **clochards** (tramps) who slept under the city's bridges and were a picturesque and not unsettling part of the tourist's view of the romantic Seine, but the situation has grown rather more severe than it was. A priest, the abbé Pierre (1912–   ), has become a popular folk hero through his work with the poor and homeless, which has included residences **(auberges Emmaüs)** for them. He and the popular comedian Coluche (1944–86) joined forces to set up the **restaurants du cœur,** soup kitchens, which provided free meals and help to the homeless.

✸

46. HUMOR

French humor is often described as being more intellectual and analytical than either English humor, which ranges from understatement and self-deprecation to silly fun, or American humor, which favors deadpan absurdity, poking fun at public figures, and veiled allusions to items of popular culture. The French have an instinctive fear of appearing ridiculous and do not like being made fun of in public.

The French word **esprit** means both "the mind" and "wit" (humor). The French enjoy telling witty anecdotes that play with words rather than sexual, dirty jokes, which are the trademark of English vaudeville comedians. An example of humorous playing with the sound of words is the series of cat drawings using the sound of the word **chat** (cat) to form many other words that contain that syllable, such as **chapeau** (hat). A similar play on sounds plays with hearers' misinterpretations, as in the "tongue"-twister (really more accurately an ear-twister), **Si six scies scient six cyprès, six cents scies scient six cents cyprès** (If six saws saw six cypresses, six hundred saws saw six hundred cypresses), which sounds like complete gibberish (**si-si-si-si-si cyprès . . .**) until the hearer identifies the word **scie.**

Another popular French comic tradition is exaggerated caricature and farce, like the mock-epic adventures of Gargantua and Pantagruel written by Rabelais (c. 1494–1553). Many popular French movies are outlandish farces that continue the Rabelaisian tradition and satirize the pretentiousness and ridiculous conventions of contemporary society.

The French enjoy comic books (**bandes dessinées, BD** for short) so much that they have elevated them to an art form. All young children know the numerous adventures of Tintin and his dog Milou, a comic strip that began in 1929. They and their parents are also avid readers of the Astérix comic books, which started in 1959. Astérix is a Gaul, like the hero Vercingetorix who led the resistance to the Roman invasion of Gaul (France). The characters besides Astérix (whose name plays on the word **astérisque**) are his robust friend Obélix (playing on **obélisque,** "obelisk"), the village poet Assurancetourix (playing on **assurance tous risques,** "comprehensive insurance"), and the tribal chief Abraracourcix (playing on **à bras raccourcis,** "with all one's force"). The adventures use settings from Roman times, but readers recognize the comic transposition of current events and attitudes in the setting, and the forays of Astérix into Roman Britain, Germany, Italy, and so on provide opportunities for readers to enjoy seeing fun poked at France's contemporary neighbors. Astérix represents the patriotic Frenchman who uses intelligence and native cunning to withstand the threats to his survival and pride from ambitious foreign countries and their ideas.

Politics has a special fascination for the French and much of their humor is politically inspired. Very popular television programs are *Le Bébête show* and *Les Guignols de l'info,* in which puppets caricature leading political personalities. Political satire has made a long-standing success of the weekly newspaper *Le Canard enchaîné.*

❁

47. IMMIGRATION

Since the French Revolution, all governments except the Vichy government during World War II have maintained the tradition of France as a country offering political asylum to all people forced to flee for safety from their homelands. During this century, France has provided homes to White Russians (Antibolsheviks); Antifascist Italians; Republican Spaniards; Jews fleeing Nazism; Hungarians, Czechs, and Slovaks fleeing reprisals after their failed attempts to oust Stalinist Communism, and Southeast Asians fleeing the dangers of Vietnam and Cambodia.

Workers from Poland and Italy have also entered France between the World Wars to work in French mines and heavy industries. Other immigrant workers, since World War II, have provided cheap labor for France's economic growth and for jobs the French didn't want to do. Africans and Arabs from France's former colonies joined Portuguese and Spaniards in forming the mass of unskilled workers in agriculture and industry. The French automobile industry in particular depended on this work force for its expansion. Since 1975 the French work force has included about 1.5 million immigrant workers, or about 6 percent of the total. The composition of the 1.5 million is 29 percent Portuguese, 16 percent Algerian, 12 percent Moroccan, 7 percent Spanish, 6 percent Italian, and 4 percent Tunisian. Some of the immigrant workers, especially those from continental Europe, are seasonal laborers who take the money they earn back to their families in their home countries.

The Arabs from Algeria, Morocco, and Tunisia are Muslim. Their large number and their different religion and customs have made them an object of racist attacks, especially by the extreme right-wing National Front party. The children of the Arabs who live in France, called **Beurs,** have for the most part been educated in French schools. They and their parents want to live permanently in France as French citizens.

A large proportion of unskilled jobs disappeared in the economic recession of the 1980s and with the growth in automation in industry. Unemployment rose dramatically. Between 1982 and 1992 unemployment among immigrant workers increased 50 percent, among French workers the increase was 29 percent. The conservative government elected in 1993 instituted an aggressive campaign of frequent police identity controls (the number of illegal immigrants is estimated to be 300,000), actively encouraged unemployed immigrants to leave the country, and introduced stricter regulations for granting French nationality to immigrants from outside the European Union. The total number of foreigners living in France is 4.5 million; it is estimated that 2 million of them are from within the European Union.

❇

48. *JE T'AIME*

Je t'aime (I love you) and **je t'adore** are frequently spoken by lovers to express their affection for each other. France and Paris have a worldwide reputation for love and romance. French people do not hide their emotions from the public gaze. Amorous encounters take place in open-air cafés. Young men openly pursue young women. And the progress of the women's movement in France has not changed young French women's expectation to be courted and paid compliments. A popular saying in France is that **l'amour** (love) rhymes with **toujours** (always) and France has given English the expression **amour fou** (madly in love).

Having a romance with a French person is an exotic fantasy for many foreigners, whose imagination is titillated by stereotypes of the French as spending their time making love, that French men are the best lovers, and that French women are the sexiest.

French history and art have helped build the exaggerated image. The twelfth-century theologian Abélard and his lover Héloïse who became a nun lived out the quintessential story of the star-crossed lovers. The leading existentialists Jean-Paul Sartre (1905–80) and Simone de Beauvoir (1908–86) carried on a lifelong open relationship before the eyes of the world. The accordion strains of many Parisian love songs have graced romantic Hollywood movies and elegant restaurants with subdued lighting. A large proportion of the French films exported to other countries have had a love plot. The Folies Bergère and the cabarets in Pigalle as well as the Lido on the Champs-Élysées and its neighbor the Crazy Horse Saloon have also made their contributions to tourists' impressions of erotic Paris.

❁

49. *JOIE DE VIVRE*

Joie de vivre (joy of living) is a French expression adopted into English. The French enjoy having fun and making the most of happy occasions. They are hardworking and serious at their professions, but during their leisure time they are keen to relax. Making time for leisurely meals and gathering with family and friends in a convivial atmosphere where work is forgotten, with plenty of jokes and laughter, is what the French understand by appreciating the quality of life.

The famous high-kicking dance, **le French can-can,** expresses the feisty abandonment of decorum in pursuit of good-tempered fun that has become an international image of French **joie de vivre.**

❁

50. KILOS

The metric system of weights and measures was invented in France. Before the Revolution, the units of measure varied from province to province. In 1790 the Constituent Assembly instructed the Academy of Sciences to establish a unit of measure that would be valid for all peoples at all times. The metric system was introduced in 1795 and became legal in 1799.

Solids are measured in **grammes, centigrammes,** and **kilogrammes** or **kilos.** The **gramme** is used for items sold in small quantities, such as spices. Several expensive items, such as meats and chocolates, have prices quoted by the **centigramme.** There are a few items (such as butter, fruit, and vegetables) sold and priced by the half kilo, which is called **une livre** (a pound).

Body weight is measured in **kilos** and **grammes.** Especially with the current fashion of exercising and diet to keep fit and slim, **kilos** is heard in this connection. **Prendre des kilos** and **perdre des kilos** means ''put on (excessive) weight'' and ''lose (excessive) weight.''

51. KISSING

Foreigners comment that the French spend a lot of time kissing each other on the cheeks. Family members and close friends, both male and female, kiss each other on both cheeks (the gesture is called **la bise**) when they meet in the morning and when they leave each other at night. The form of **la bise** varies from region to region: one kiss on each cheek, one kiss on one cheek and two on the other, or twice on both cheeks.

On formal occasions men of the upper bourgeoisie and aristocracy may kiss the hand of a married woman instead of shaking her hand to greet and say farewell. The custom is disappearing along with other rules of rigid etiquette.

Kissing on the lips is erotic and is only for lovers.

Some language notes are in order. The verb for ''to kiss'' is **embrasser,** or **s'embrasser** ''to kiss each other.'' The noun is **un baiser.** There is a verb **baiser** that often confuses foreigners because the French never use it to mean ''to kiss''; rather, it means ''to have sex.''

52. LEISURE

The French workweek has been reduced to 38 hours and the legal retirement age to 60, and French leisure time has increased as a result. So far, the increase in leisure time has largely meant more time watching television. The adult population is estimated to spend six hours a day on media leisure activities (which are sometimes done simultaneously): 37 minutes reading newspapers and magazines, 1 hour 59 minutes listening to the radio, and 3 hours 19 minutes watching television. Average daily household television-viewing time in 1993 in the United States was 6 hours, 39 minutes, in the summer month of July and 7 hours, 32 minutes, in November.

Every French person in 1992 spent an average of 5,124 francs on leisure activities apart from vacations. This was an increase of 5.5 percent since 1960. Only the money spent on health showed a higher increase.

Leisure activities can be divided between cultural pursuits (such as reading, listening to music, going to the movies, theater, and concerts, visiting museums and art exhibitions, and photography) and simple relaxation activities (such as sports, forest and mountain walks, fishing, hunting, playing cards, dancing in clubs, gardening, doing house repairs). The French rarely concentrate on only one of these two types of leisure activities. They mix both in accordance with the precept of the sixteenth-century epicurean philosopher Michel de Montaigne (1533–92) that an active mind needs to be balanced by a healthy body. Among cultural leisure pursuits, audiovisual activities (television, videocassettes, movies, listening to music) have become increasingly popular.

French men report that 80 percent of them do household repairs and 60 percent of all French people do some form of gardening. The French are keen collectors and 23 percent of the population over the age of 15 have some kind of collection, the largest group (8 percent) being stamp collectors. There is a photo camera in 90 percent of French homes and a video camera in 10 percent. The earliest photographic processes were French, by the way. Nicéphore Niepce (1765–1833) developed a process in 1826 and Louis Jacques Daguerre (1787–1851), for whom the daguerreotype was named, refined it and sold the patent to the state in 1839.

❁

53. *LIBERTÉ, ÉGALITÉ, FRATERNITÉ*

"Liberty, equality, fraternity" was the rallying cry of the French Revolutionaries who brought an end to the oppression, inequalities, and privileges of the absolute monarchy. The slogan originated when the *Journal de Paris* appealed to the public to print these words on their homes. The French Republic took up the slogan and has always seen the defense of individual liberties as one of its basic principles. **Fraternité** has come to mean mutual support of all groups in the community. That is, it is roughly synonymous with solidarity.

Many national independence movements of the nineteenth and twentieth centuries have adopted the slogan in their struggles to overthrow oppressive regimes.

❁

54. LOGIC

The French pride themselves in being logical in their thinking and rational in their behavior, a characteristic that traces back to the French philosopher René Descartes (1596–1650), who postulated that intellect is humanity's distinguishing characteristic. Descartes's radical reduction of evidence in his philosophy to **Je pense, donc je suis** (I think, therefore I am) began an analytical tradition known as Cartesian logic. Voltaire (1694–1778) and other eighteenth-century philosophers who inspired the Age of Enlightenment that subjected all fields of social and political endeavor to critical inquiry drew on Cartesian principles. This form of rationalism has continued as a dominant strain in French philosophy to the present time.

The Cartesian influence can be seen in many aspects of French life. Young children who misbehave are told to be **raisonnable** (reasonable). Schools practice a rational approach to learning and stress the ability to memorize, think clearly, and discuss abstract ideas. High intellectual performance is valued above sporting or civic achievements. The final high school examination, **le baccalauréat,** has philosophy as one of the literary subjects and emphasizes rhetorical skills and deductive reasoning.

Intellectuals form a distinctive group in French society. They are admired for their abstract knowledge and their skill in challenging existing beliefs. They are also respected opinion makers and news media often publish or broadcast interviews with them.

It has been said that the French prefer the exchange of ideas and a long discussion about the theoretical principles of a project to making a decision to act; that the educational system that favors intellectual over practical and vocational outcomes has restricted France's development in industry, commerce, and technology; that more pragmatic peoples can achieve consensus more efficiently, since French discussions bring about ideological conflicts that delay decision making. The French would object that by daring to be different and by challenging solutions based on mere expediency they are having a positive influence on the way the world thinks.

✵

55. MARRIAGE AND DIVORCE

French couples often celebrate two separate marriage ceremonies because of the separation of Church and State that has existed since 1905. The civil ceremony is obligatory and takes place at the city hall **(mairie).** The marriage assumes legal status by this ceremony, which the mayor records in the **livret de famille** (family booklet) given to the newlyweds. The couple's children will be recorded in the **livret,** giving the children legal status. If the couple wants a church marriage, it follows the civil ceremony.

France has the lowest per capita marriage rate in Europe; it decreased by half between 1972 and 1987 and increased only slightly after 1987. The number of unmarried couples living together increased during this period and the average age of marriage rose for women from 22.4 to 25.7 and for men from 24.4 to 27.8. The marriages in which one marriage partner was not French increased from 6 percent in 1970 to 14 percent in 1993. At the same time, divorces almost tripled over the last twenty years. Today almost one-third of French marriages end in divorce, 45 percent of them citing unfaithfulness as the reason for the divorce.

Today 12 percent of the total population and 20 percent of those between 18 and 24 years old live together as unmarried couples. In 1976, 62 percent of the population were shocked by unmarried cohabitation; today fewer than 30 percent are. The growing public tolerance toward unmarried couples extends to their children, who now number 30 percent of all babies born. The law allows unmarried couples to assign to each other certain legal rights, including social security benefits, by declaring their relationship at city hall. The right to inherit each other's property, however, they cannot so assign.

Marriage is no longer seen as a religious and social institution but as a personal decision. Despite the lower marriage rate, the growing divorce rate, the growing number of unmarried couples cohabiting, and the increase in single-parent families, 69 percent of French people in 1991 still agreed that ''the family is the place where you can feel comfortable and relaxed'' and only 13 percent agreed that ''people should no longer get married.''

❁

56. *LA MARSEILLAISE*

The French national anthem was originally a war march composed in 1792 by Captain Claude Rouget de Lisle (1760–1836) while he was garrisoned in Strasbourg. The Marseilles National Guard sang it as they entered Paris in July of that year, inspiring French patriotism with its stirring music, and thus it became known as **''La Marseillaise.''** The opening two lines are

> **Allons, enfants de la patrie**
> **Le jour de gloire est arrivé.**
> Let's go, children of the homeland
> The day of glory has arrived.

The battle call is repeated in each refrain:

> **Aux armes, citoyens! Formez vos bataillons!**
> **Marchons! Marchons!**
> Take your weapons, citizens! Form your battalions!
> Let's march! Let's march!

Napoleon's (1769–1821) victorious armies made the French national anthem famous across Europe. Today, two centuries after its composition, it still symbolizes revolutionary fervor and patriotism for the French wherever they are in the world and especially on their national day on July 14.

57. MEALS

Dinner **(le dîner)** is the main French meal of the day. Lunch **(le déjeuner)** is also important but assumes second place, especially since the traditional two-hour lunch break is being replaced in cities by a one-hour lunch. Sunday lunch remains a long meal at which family and friends often gather. Breakfast **(le petit déjeuner)** is a rapid meal often consisting of only bread and jam with a bowl of coffee. Only young children tend to have any snacks between meals, and even that is formalized as the after-school **goûter.**

The main meals have several courses, accompanied by lots of bread and mineral water or wine. The beginning, **hors d'œuvre,** which for dinner is often soup, is followed by the main course of meat with vegetables or pasta, followed by green salad or cheese (a source of national pride) and fruit or dessert.

Simple main courses are steak and fries **(biftek frites)** or chicken and fries **(poulet frites).** Other favorites are blanquette of veal **(blanquette de veau)** with rice, chicken in red wine **(coq au vin)** with boiled potatoes, and beef stew **(pot au feu)** with mixed vegetables.

The range of courses will strike an American as unusual. Visitors to France should prepare to be surprised with dishes such as **la bouillabaisse** (fish soup), **les endives** (Belgian endive, or what the English know as chicory), **les asperges** (asparagus), **le boudin blanc** (a delicately flavored white sausage similar to the German bockwurst), or **le lapin** (rabbit).

Mealtimes traditionally are a family affair at which parents and children discuss the day's events at school and at work. Some French families follow the modern trend of leaving the television on during meals, to the detriment of conversation.

Table manners are generally more formal than in America, with wrists and arms resting on the edge of the table and not in the lap. Americans might be surprised during the meal to see the fork replace the knife in the right hand and a small piece of bread used by the left hand and to push food onto the fork before it is carried to the mouth. When the main course is served, you are expected to begin eating it while it is hot and not wait until everyone is served. Bread-and-butter plates are not used. The crusty French bread is placed on the table beside the plate you eat from. Bread is not eaten with butter or margarine; butter is served only with some cheeses. The same plate, after being wiped clean with bread, is used for the lettuce salad after the main course, but a new plate is usually used for cheese if it is not separated from the main course by a lettuce salad. A knife and fork are always used in a restaurant, and often at home, to peel and eat fruit such as apples for dessert.

❁

58. MEDIA

The adult French population spends an average of 3 hours 19 minutes a day watching television, of which 49 minutes is for soap operas, 24 minutes for news, 20 minutes for documentaries, 17 minutes for movies, 16 minutes each for game shows and variety shows, 12 minutes for advertisements, and 8 minutes for sports.

The majority of the seven French television channels are administered by the state. The most popular channels are the state-owned **A2** and the privately owned **TF1**. Channel **M6** shows rock music clips. Channel **Arte** shows high-culture programs from France and Germany. There is one pay television channel, **Canal-Plus**, which shows mainly recent and classical movies. Satellite television allows the French to watch programs shown on the television channels of other European countries.

French tastes can show contrasts, as demonstrated by the mass appeal of serials **(les feuilletons)**—which are often American imports—game shows, and serious political interview programs such as *L'Heure de Vérité*.

The French spend on average 1 hour 59 minutes listening to the radio, whose largest stations are again owned by the state. The most popular commercial stations are **RTL (Radio Luxembourg), Europe 1**, and **RMC (Radio Monte Carlo)**. Community radio stations called **radios libres** broadcast programs to specific groups of younger and older listeners.

The state subsidizes some small-circulation newspapers such as the communist national daily *L'Humanité* in order to maintain a diversity of opinion in the press. National and regional newspapers tend to align with the views of a political party. The extensive Robert Hersant group, of which *Le Figaro* is the flagship, offers conservative views and analyses to its large bourgeois readership. Readers follow progressive and radical opinions in *Libération. Le Monde* is a serious thinking newspaper that claims objectivity in its presentation of a diverse range of opinions designed to stimulate intellectual debate. Papers devote a great deal of space to politics.

Five national magazines published at the end of each week for weekend reading exert considerable influence on opinions, attitudes, and tastes: the conservative *Le Point,* the liberal *L'Express,* the radical *L'Événement du jeudi,* the socialist *Le Nouvel Observateur,* and the bourgeois *Le Figaro Magazine.* The last, published in conjunction with the Saturday edition of *Le Figaro,* appeals like the newspaper to the new bourgeois consumer class. Numerous magazines for women, youth, and special interests are also published. The largest-selling of all French magazines is the weekly television guide, *Télé 7 Jours.*

❁

59. MEN AND WOMEN

The traditional French role for the man was the breadwinner and the one with the power and authority to make all family decisions. In the working classes many women have always worked. (Traditionally their husbands gave them their pay packets and they were responsible for the family budget.) In all classes women were responsible for the children's education.

A large percentage of upper-class women have been continuing their studies to a higher level and now want to have a career in management like men. The greater percentage of French women entering the work force is influencing family life, and men's role is changing. In 1972 a law was passed establishing equal salaries for men and women.

In 1974 Simone Veil, the Minister for Health, legalized contraception, which gave women a new freedom, and in the same year a ministerial post for women's affairs (**Secrétariat d'État de la Condition Féminine**) was established. Françoise Giroud assumed the post and proposed that for biological reasons women should seek equivalent rather than identical status with men. In 1975 a divorce reform made it possible for the first time to divorce by mutual consent.

In 1990, 59.2 percent of women were in the work force and 76 percent of men. Greater financial and reproductive independence made it easier for women to free themselves from the domination of men. In 1991 the socialist president François Mitterrand (1916–   ) appointed France's first woman prime minister, Édith Cresson (1934–   ), but she became a scapegoat for the declining popularity of the socialist government in general and held office for only ten months. Household and family duties have come to be shared to a greater extent, despite the fact that French men, like those of Mediterranean Europe, have been slower than men in Northern Europe to share these chores with their wives.

French women, in winning equivalent status with men, seem to foreign observers to have been able to keep their reputation for femininity and fashionable dress sense.

Male chauvinist attitudes that are slower to change in many aspects of daily life are not as evident in intellectual discussions, where women's opinions receive the same respect as men's. Men and women from the same social class treat each other as intellectually equal, and discussions are mutual.

The symbol of the French Republic is a woman, Marianne. Her image appears on bank bills, coins, and stamps. Every French city hall (**mairie**) displays a head-and-shoulders statue of her.

✖

60. MONEY

The units of currency are the **franc** and the **centime.** One **franc** equals 100 **centimes.** Older people often calculate amounts in **anciens francs,** the inflated franc before it was devalued 1:100 by Charles de Gaulle (1890–1970) when he came to power in 1958.

The European unit of currency is the **écu,** which is used in commercial transactions between countries in the European Union. English speakers should remember that **la monnaie** means change or small coins and not money, which is **l'argent.** "Cash" is **l'argent liquide.**

Until recently the French frequently used personal checks to pay for purchases in supermarkets and shops. The proprietors could accept checks with some confidence because, under French law, to give a worthless check is punishable by a large fine or imprisonment. Credit cards have become more common lately, the most common of which is the **Carte Bleue,** which the French can also use abroad.

It took some time for the French to accept the use of credit to buy consumer items. The French tradition was to keep as much money as possible in savings **(l'épargne)** and spend it only on essential items. At the same time, the French nurtured a mistrust of the banking system, and it was not uncommon for wealthy peasants and prudent bourgeois to convert savings into gold coin and hide it at home in a woolen sock. These habits gave the French a reputation for being stingy and reluctant to spend money without compelling reasons. Even today, the French demand value for their money and expect their purchases to last. They may have joined the consumer society, but not the throw-away society.

France has a wider disparity in income between the rich and the poor than most other European countries. The top 1 percent of the French population possesses 20 percent of the nation's private wealth, and the bottom 10 percent have 0.1 percent. The wage difference between a senior manager and an unskilled worker is approximately 7:1.

The French are mainly conservative about money and do not flaunt their wealth. The wealthy invest their money discreetly in property and cultural artifacts such as antiques, old paintings, and tapestries, and by these means acquire respect and status among the

63

bourgeoisie. Money was a taboo topic of conversation until the 1980s. During that decade the fortunes amassed by flamboyant entrepreneurs like Bernard Tapie (1945–   ) inspired volumes of media coverage. Such entrepreneurs were called the "golden boys" because of the success of their stock raids and takeovers. Their ostentation shocked the mainly conservative French. The continuing recession of the early 1990s brought collapse to the fortunes of the golden boys.

Napoleon Bonaparte (1769–1821) instituted inheritance laws to keep wealth within the family, and his laws are still in force. The law dictates that a father's estate be bequeathed to children in equal shares. The law has created a patchwork of the French countryside, especially in prosperous farming areas such as Normandy, for family farms have been repeatedly divided into smaller and smaller plots through inheritance and recombined somewhat randomly through marriage. (An unspoken calculation in many rural marriages is the resulting tenure the couple will hold when the lands are combined.) Another result has been that city dwellers will often own a small lot of inherited land in the country and perhaps a country house that they share jointly with the families of their brothers and sisters.

❁

61. NAMES AND NAME DAYS

France is a traditionally Catholic country, and so the majority of first names are taken from the Catholic calendar of saints' names. Children celebrate their birthday (**anniversaire**) and also their feast day (**fête**) on the feast of the saint after whom they are named.

Until 1992 state law recommended that children be given a name from a roster of names. Parents being parents, they sought to give their children individuality by forming more original names by hyphenated combination, such as Marie-Françoise and Jean-Pierre. Some French names are "unisex": Camille, Claude, and Dominique, for example.

The most frequent French family names are Martin, Bernard, Moreau, Durand, and Petit. Dupont, frequently treated as the typical French family name, actually ranks fifteenth in frequency.

The particle **de** before a family name indicates that the family belonged to the nobility or wishes to give the impression that it did. Adult members of the family usually wear a signet ring stamped with the family crest. Despite France's being a republic, families with a **de** name enjoy a certain social prestige. Those descended from noble families who lived before the 1789 Revolution have more prestige than those whose families bought the title since then. President Giscard d'Estaing's (1926–   ) father acquired the noble title ''d'Estaing'' in 1922 after proving that his family owned the castle where the d'Estaing family to whom he claimed he was related had lived.

❁

62. NUMBERS

The French use of numbers is more than a matter of translation, and knowing about French numbering style can be useful not only for making sure of getting correct change in shops and restaurants but also in understanding the distance to be traveled, in taking down telephone numbers, and in several unexpected situations.

French telephone numbers have eight digits, which are not recited singly but in pairs: 43-12-95-06, **quarante-trois, douze, quatre-vingt-quinze, zéro six.**

France is officially divided into ninety-five administrative districts called **départements.** Each one has a number as well as a name. For example, the Ain **département** in the Rhône-Alpes region is 01, the city of Paris is 75, and the Val d'Oise **département** in the Paris region is 95. The numbers serve as the beginning of the **département** postal codes and terminate license plate numbers of cars registered in the **département.** French drivers know to beware of vehicles displaying 75 on their license plates because of the disrespect of Parisian drivers for slow drivers and for conventional safety rules.

Some handwritten French numerals look different from the corresponding American ones. A French 1 looks like a capital A without the cross bar, and a French 7 is crossed with a bar to avoid confusion with a 1. To Americans, French use of commas and periods in numbers seems reversed. A comma is used to indicate decimals, as in the price **F2,30** (two francs, thirty centimes; sometimes written **2F30**) or

54,5 pour cent (54.5 percent). A period sometimes separates numbers above one thousand into groups of three digits (**6.819** for six thousand eight hundred nineteen), although spaces are more common: **57 287 212 habitants** (57,287,212 inhabitants).

The street-level floor of a building is called the **rez-de-chaussée,** not the first floor **(le premier étage),** which is the floor above the street level. The French defend their logic by saying that the street level is not a story.

The French observe some conventions in counting days that can cause unwary travelers some problems. A week is **huit jours,** and two weeks is **quinze jours.** Therefore a Eurail pass for **huit jours** is actually valid for only seven days. One British traveler nearly came to blows with a French conductor over the issue. Sure of his arithmetic, the exasperated traveler insisted on taking the number literally and loudly counted out the days on which the pass was valid. The equally exasperated conductor tried to force the French idea into the British head without success. Neither **sang-froid** (cool-bloodedness) nor stiff upper lip were maintained on that occasion.

✪

63. OVERSEAS DEPARTMENTS AND TERRITORIES

Charles de Gaulle (1890–1970) granted independence to France's last colonies when he returned to power in 1958. The French influence nevertheless remains obvious in the former African colonies of **Cameroun, Congo, Côte d'Ivoire, Gabon, Guinée, Niger, Mali, Sénégal, Tchad,** and **Togo,** and the French for their part maintain a close emotional attachment to events in those countries.

Certain lands overseas still belong to France. France proper **(la France métropolitaine),** which includes the Mediterranean island of Corsica, is distinguished from **la France d'outre-mer** (overseas France), which is administratively divided into **départements d'outre-mer (DOM)** and **territoires d'outre-mer (TOM).**

The **DOM** (overseas departments) are **Guadeloupe, Guyane française, Martinique, Saint-Pierre-et-Miquelon** off the coast of

FRENCH-SPEAKING COUNTRIES OF AFRICA

Newfoundland in Canada, and **Réunion** in the Indian Ocean. They have equal status with mainland French **départements** and send representatives to the National Assembly. The **TOM** (overseas territories) are **Mayotte** in the Indian Ocean, and **Polynésie française, Nouvelle-Calédonie,** and **Wallis-et-Futuna** in the Pacific Ocean, as well as other minor archipelagoes. Their inhabitants have full French citizenship and elected local governments. Some territories have growing independence movements.

64. PARIS

Since the celebration of the bicentenary of the French Revolution in 1989, France has attracted more tourists annually than any other country. (The United States ranks second.) In 1992 the number of tourists to France exceeded its population of 57 million. Most tourists visit Paris, the capital, which many claim to be the most beautiful city in the world. Part of the city's beauty derives from its wide avenues, the Seine riverfront, and the height limit of seven stories on its gracious old buildings, which gives the city skyline a harmonious appearance. Paris sits on the right (north) and left (south) banks of the Seine.

The center of Paris is the **Île de la Cité,** originally a village established in 200 BC by the Parisii, a Gallic tribe, and conquered by the

The Arrondissements of Paris

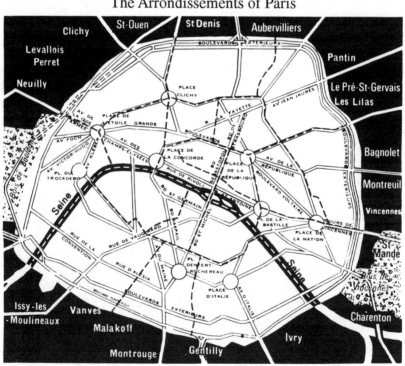

Romans in 52 BC. The famous Gothic cathedral of **Notre-Dame de Paris** on this island serves as a visual and cultural focal point of the city and is the scene of important national memorial ceremonies. The boulevards interconnect the city's many **places** (roughly, ''squares,'' although they are circular) that act as neighborhood landmarks and sites of chaotic traffic competition. The circular **Boulevard Périphérique** separates Paris from its suburbs **(la banlieue).**

The underground **métro** with its numerous stations makes travel around the city easy for residents as well as for the tourists who come to admire the treasure-filled museums like the **Louvre**, the **Musée d'Orsay**, and the **Centre Pompidou**; to wander the historical precincts of the Latin Quarter, **Montmartre**, and the **Champs-Élysées**; to drink coffee in the cafés of **St-Germain-des-Prés**; and to dine in the restaurants of **Montparnasse** or shop in the trendy fashion boutiques of the left bank.

The new business center of Paris is outside the city limits in the western suburb of **La Défense**, whose **Grande Arche**, inaugurated for the bicentenary, stands at one end of a majestic perspective that passes through the **Arc de Triomphe** and the **Place de la Concorde** to the Louvre at its other end.

By a change in its administrative status, Paris was allowed to elect a mayor in 1977 for the first time since 1871. The **Commune de Paris,** a workers' revolutionary movement, in that year tried to make Paris independent of French government control after the Prussians invaded the city during the Franco-Prussian War. Consequently the central government was for a hundred years wary of granting Paris too much autonomy. The Gaullist Jacques Chirac (1932–) was the winner of the 1977 mayoral election, and under his administration the city has been cleaner and public services more efficient. Because of the prestige Paris gives him, the mayor is seen as a rival to the influence the president of the Republic can have over the capital city.

French government has long been quite centralized, and despite recent reforms encouraging decentralization Paris remains the political, administrative, financial, and cultural center of the nation in the hearts of the French and by administrative habit.

❁

65. PARISIANS

Parisians have a reputation for believing themselves superior to all non-Parisians in France and throughout the world. Their candid opinions about the virtues of life in Paris strike many outsiders as undisguised arrogance. The stereotypical Parisian sees the entire world as revolving around Paris and awaiting its judgments before adopting new fashions and attitudes. The beautiful atmosphere of light that bathes the city in spring and fall and the elegant nightly illuminations of Parisian monuments and historic facades have given birth to the epithet **la ville lumière** (city of light) for the city; non-Parisians scoff that Parisians commonly misinterpret the epithet to refer to the intellectual and cultural enlightenment that Paris bestows on the world.

Parisians of course are a mixed group of people as are the people of all major capitals. Their lives are often stressful as they struggle with traffic jams, inadequate housing, crowds, limited facilities for relaxation, and city regulations. Many Parisians maintain strong links with country regions from which they or their families came. The wealthy of the **beaux quartiers** (upper-class neighborhoods) can escape to their weekend country houses and recoup their energies for the next week of hectic Parisian life, but the working classes (whose neighborhoods are under pressure from gentrification) and the large North African population of **Belleville** and **Goutte d'Or** cannot afford weekend retreats and must content themselves with Sunday afternoons walking the streets and sitting in public parks or cafés. These poor classes might go to the movies, but they rarely participate in the abundance of cultural activities for which Paris is famous around the world. There is a growing trend for some married Parisians with young children to leave the stress of the capital to work in large regional towns, which offer a higher quality of family life. However, Parisians, like the French in general, make career moves to other cities and regions much less than Americans.

❁

66. POLITENESS AND DIRECTNESS

Foreigners sometimes find the French rude and dismissive. One reason is the directness and frankness with which they express their feelings and opinions. They are accustomed to speaking their minds with each other without fear of offending the listener and expect their listeners to respond with equal candor. Another contributing factor is the strong professional and social hierarchy in France whose expression in French attitudes strikes foreigners from more egalitarian societies as patronizing.

With each other the French are sociable. They constantly greet each other, shake one another's hand, and exchange tokens of politeness. Customers entering small shops greet shopkeepers with **Bonjour, Messieurs-Dames** (roughly equivalent to "Good day, ladies and gentlemen") and depart with **Au revoir, Messieurs-Dames.** One person's **Merci** (thank you) is always acknowledged with **Je vous en prie** or **Je t'en prie** (you're welcome) or the less formal **De rien** (don't mention it). People eating together offer **Bon appétit** to each other. **Pardon** (excuse me) begins a request to an acquaintance for information or to a stranger for street directions. Passing ahead of another person in going through a door or squeezing past in a crowd is also excused with a **Pardon.** When the French see occasion for a personal criticism, the comment is always preceded with an apology, which they see as transforming the criticism into a polite observation rather than a personal attack.

People use professional titles in conversation, when they are applicable, to signify polite respect: **Monsieur le Directeur/Madame la Directrice; Monsieur/Madame le Docteur; Maître** (for an attorney or a famous artist); **Monsieur le Curé/Mon Père/Ma Sœur; Monsieur le Pasteur; Monsieur/Madame le Professeur; Monsieur/Madame le Maire.**

In the 1970s the government became concerned that a French reputation for rudeness was discouraging the influx of tourist income, which makes a significant contribution to the national economy. They launched a campaign asking the French to be polite and welcoming to tourists. The French began to try to communicate with tourists in their native languages and not insist on speaking French with them, as had been their custom. The reorientation accompanied a shift by the French to a more international perspective on France's position in the world.

❁

67. *QUEUES* (LINES)

The English may set a world standard for the orderliness of their lines at bus stops, taxi stands, and ticket windows, which they take as a manifestation of their civic responsibility and polite respect for each other. French behavior suggests that they do not accept the English standard in this matter as in so many others.

French lines are disorderly affairs, and everyone seems to have a logical personal reason to go to the front of the line. Lines publicly demonstrate the single-minded French devotion to individualism and reluctance to acquiesce to any group enterprise that smacks of homo-geneity. It is a national pastime to find a way around a government regulation or administrative decision, and the name of this national pastime is **le système D,** an expression that has much to say about French temperament.

The **D** stands for **débrouillard,** which, translated most simply, means "resourceful" but implies a great deal more. The literal mean-ing of **débrouiller** is "to untangle," and so from the French point of view, the chaos of a French line is the logical consequence of a mass of individuals untangling the knotty problem of getting to the head of the line. The French practice **la débrouillardise** in all aspects of life, whether it be in getting a broken electrical appliance to work, in jumping a line, or in finding a way to pay less tax. The French compli-ment **il/elle sait se débrouiller** (he/she knows how to get things done) is always sincere and always accompanied with a twinkle in the eye.

❁

68. REGIONALIZATION

France is a highly centralized country in which the administrative structures are very hierarchical, and all major national decisions are made in Paris. At the local level, France is divided into 36,000 **communes**. Each **commune** has a municipal council, which elects a mayor **(le maire)**. The **communes** are grouped in 95 **départements,** whose head is a **préfet (préfète)** appointed by the national government. The capital **(chef-lieu)** of each **département** houses its administrative offices and the **préfet (préfète)**. The **départements** themselves are grouped into 22 **régions** whose administrative head is a **préfet (préfète) de région,** also appointed from Paris. The names of the **régions** correspond to those of the provinces that covered similar areas before the 1789 Revolution, for example, **Picardie, Bourgogne** (Burgundy), **Auvergne, Provence-Alpes-Côte d'Azur.**

The hierarchical relation between Paris and "the provinces" explains how the capital dominates the country and why Parisians consider themselves superior to the "provincials." Charles de Gaulle (1890–1970) had tried to give more autonomy to the regions, but the referendum of 1969 to approve administrative reforms lost, upon which de Gaulle resigned his presidency. The socialist government of François Mitterrand (1916–96) elected in 1981 did succeed in putting into effect a reformist program of decentralization. The program provided for elected regional councils with power to make certain financial and local policy decisions without authorization from Paris or the government appointed **préfet.** The new autonomy allowed the regions to develop their own resources and identity within the European Economic Community, and regional centers such as Lyon and Toulouse grew rapidly as key centers within the European commercial network.

Despite the reforms, Paris continues to exert a broad influence on all aspects of French life, for the centralizing mentality that established the administrative, political, economic, and cultural preeminence of Paris had been entrenched for centuries. Decades of conscious efforts to regionalize policies and establish functioning regional institutions will be necessary to overcome tradition and the arguments of Parisian centralists who can point to the many national benefits that have resulted from state planning and control, such as the Euro Tunnel under the English Channel, the nuclear power grid, and the TGV **(train à grande vitesse).**

❁

69. RELIGION

Eighty percent of the French people say they are Catholic, but 42 percent of that number do not practice their religion, and only 8 percent go to church every week. Fifteen percent of the French say they are nonbelievers. The decline in church attendance and church influence on daily life has accelerated with the progress of consumerist values since the 1960s. Much of French history and tradition, however, are closely bound up with a Catholic identity.

Since Clovis (465–511), the king of the Francs, converted to Catholicism in AD 496 and made Paris the royal capital, the Catholic tradition has been glorified in abbeys and churches throughout France. The soaring height and devout sculptures and stained-glass scenes of France's medieval Gothic cathedrals are concrete evidence of the fervent religious faith of the twelfth through fifteenth centuries. Catholicism began so early and was so visible in French life that France was called the eldest daughter of the church of Rome.

French saints have been some of the most effective and influential in the world. St. Francis de Sales (1567–1622) reestablished the forgotten principle that salvation was for everyone, not just for the clergy. The charity work of St. Vincent de Paul (1581–1660) among the poor caused a small revolution in French society; his work is continued by his followers in many countries today. More than 5 million pilgrims each year visit the grotto of St. Bernadette (1844–79) in Lourdes (Pyrénées), an estimated half million of them in hopes of a miraculous cure of physical disabilities.

France was one of the first countries to experience the conflicts of the Protestant Reformation in the sixteenth century. The Wars of Religion (1562–98) saw fierce battles between the French Protestants **(Huguenots)** and Catholics. The Edict of Nantes, promulgated in 1598 by Henri IV (1553–1610), the Protestant king who converted to Catholicism to stop the religious fighting, gave Protestants the legal right to practice their religion and granted them certain cities as safe havens. King Louis XIV (1638–1715), seeing the free cities as a threat to the absolute royal power he was trying to establish, revoked the edict in 1685, and more than 250,000 French Protestants emigrated to The Netherlands, Germany, and Switzerland. Today Protestants constitute 2 percent of the French population and reside mainly in the East (Alsace) and the South (Languedoc).

The French Revolution of 1789 attacked the privileges and wealth of the Catholic Church, and the church and the Republican state were adversaries for a century. In 1905 the Third Republic separated church and state by law, defusing the conflict. Since that time French republics have been constitutionally secular and make no reference to God or religion in state ceremonies. The lay tradition (la laïcité) had many vocal adherents among republicans opposed to the church hierarchy, especially among teachers when primary schooling became obligatory for all French children in 1882. State financial aid to private schools (most of which are Catholic) is a subject that reopens the unresolved and volatile issues of a nominally Catholic population that is secular in its behavior with a nominally secular government that is Catholic in its philosophical assumptions.

The second-largest religion after Catholicism in France today is not Protestantism, but Islam. France has more than 900 mosques for the large number of practicing Muslims among the North African immigrants and their families. More than a quarter of France's mosques are in and around Paris.

Jews constitute 1 percent of the total French population, the highest percentage in Western Europe. More than half of them live in Paris. Not that France has been at all times a congenial haven for Jews. Ultranationalist sentiments were quite pronounced in late-nineteenth-century France, and these sentiments contributed to unfair conduct in the 1894 trial of a Jewish army officer, Alfred Dreyfus (1859–1935), who was falsely convicted of espionage. Republicans fought hard to defend the innocence of Dreyfus, who was finally cleared of all accusations in 1906. Many French Jews died in Nazi concentration camps during the German occupation of 1940–44, often with official French complicity.

❁

70. REPUBLIC

The First French Republic, founded in 1792, arose after the French Revolution of 1789 in which the middle class, the peasants, and the working class rose against the absolute powers of the monarchy and the excessive privileges of the aristocracy. These events marked the end of the **Ancien Régime** and the beginning of modern democratic France.

The Declaration of the Rights of Man and of the Citizen expressed the guiding principles of the new republic. The declaration embodied the reformist ideals of the eighteenth-century Enlightenment philosophers: equality of all by nature and in the eyes of the law; the obligation of government to guarantee equality, liberty, safety, and property; the separation of legislative, executive, and judicial powers, the basis of good government according to the philosophy of Montesquieu (1689–1755).

The symbolic collapse of the **Ancien Régime** was the fall of the Bastille on July 14, 1789, only seventy-five days after George Washington took office as the first president of the United States under a republican constitution influenced by the very same Enlightenment principles as the French First Republic. In the two centuries since, a single republic has formed the government of the United States and France has lived through five republics, a constitutional monarchy, and two empires. Three of the five republics were heralded by the revolutionary cry **Aux barricades!** (To the barricades!)

A student revolt in May 1968 against outmoded university structures, which raised questions about rigid state controls in general, finally erupted into a general national workers' strike and violent confrontations with police that brought General Charles de Gaulle's (1890–1970) government to the brink of collapse. Salaries were raised, working conditions were improved, workers gained a voice in work-place decisions, and many other state controls on work, education, and other areas of French life were relaxed as a result. The same social changes had appeared in other western countries without the violent confrontations. Significant political and social changes in France seem to come about more from explosive ideological conflict than from smooth evolutionary change.

The First Republic (1792–1804) lasted until Napoleon Bonaparte (1769–1821) proclaimed the First Empire. Imperial though they were, victorious Napoleonic armies carried the ideals of the Revolution throughout Europe and sowed the seeds for democratic government in much of twentieth-century Europe.

After Napoleon's defeat, a constitutional monarchy reigned until the Second Republic (1848–52) abolished it. Napoleon III

(1808–73), in turn, ended the Second Republic and established the Second Empire (1852–70).

Napoleon III was defeated by an invading Prussian army, an event that established at one blow the first unified Germany in history and the Third French Republic. The new German Empire promptly annexed Alsace and Lorraine, lands that through much of history have served as a first-place trophy whenever Germany and France have opposed each other in a military contest. A working-class insurrection in Paris **(la Commune de Paris)** during the invasion had hoped to establish a more radical government, but the new Third Republic (1870–1940) repressed the movement violently, survived World War I (reclaiming Alsace and Lorraine as the victor in 1918), and saw its political institutions endure until Hitler's successful military invasion in 1940 during World War II.

The Fourth Republic was established after the end of the war, in 1946. It lasted until 1958, when Charles de Gaulle (1890–1970) was recalled to lead France with a new constitution giving the president more power than Parliament and establishing the Fifth Republic. The new constitution gave France a stability that continues today.

All five French Republics have paid homage to the democratic principles of the 1789 Revolution, and the Republican slogan, **Liberté, Égalité, Fraternité,** has become a constant in the rhetoric of all modern French political parties. The traditional conclusion of official presidential addresses to the French people is **Vive la République! Vive la France!** (Long live the Republic! Long live France!) The French may nurse a popular fascination with the lives of the British royal family, but republican sentiment runs very deep in French society and determines both national and international attitudes of the French. A distinctive and constant feature of French foreign policy is the condemnation of totalitarian regimes that restrict individual liberties and freedom of speech.

❋

71. RIGHTS

The French trace the beginning of their modern country to the Declaration of the Rights of Man and of the Citizen (1789), much as Americans trace theirs to the Declaration of Independence in 1776. The declaration, inspired by the ideas of the eighteenth-century Enlightenment philosophers, granted all French citizens equality in nature and in the eyes of the law. The fact that an individual's rights were first enshrined in a Revolutionary declaration could explain why French citizens are quick to assert their individual rights whenever they think they are being threatened. Sometimes it is simply affronted dignity that produces the rebuke **Tu n'as pas le droit de faire ça!** (You don't have the right to do that!) or **J'ai le droit de . . .** (I have the right to . . .). This spontaneous reaction can be heard in many daily life contexts ranging from parents admonishing children to people jostling each other to move forward in a crowd or a line of impatient drivers trying to cut off other drivers in heavy traffic. It is often frequently heard in offices. One of the many official cards and documents carried by French citizens is often required to be shown to public administration officers as proof of permanent rights. However, the document is valid only if it bears an official stamp!

Under the Napoleonic Code, incidentally, the principle of law is that the accused is presumed guilty until proven innocent.

72. SHOPPING

Shopping in France incorporates remembrances of the past with foretastes of the future, for small village centers still support some specialty shops, street markets even in large cities maintain an unbroken tradition from centuries past, and even rural shopping includes forays into huge hypermarkets on city outskirts. However, unlike Americans, the French do not go to shopping malls for leisure and entertainment.

Local shops **(boutiques)** and street markets **(marchés en plein air)** are in many ways the most authentic taste of France: **la boulangerie** (bread bakery), **la pâtisserie** (pastry shop), **la charcuterie** (delicatessen), and **l'épicerie** (grocery) among the everyday and **la librairie** (bookshop) and **la joaillerie-horlogerie** (jewelry and clock shop) among the more specialized. In small shops, the encounter is a personal one. Customer and shopkeeper exchange greetings as the customer enters and leaves. Initial reaction to supermarkets was negative because the service in them was impersonal.

Exchanges at the street markets, usually held twice a week in towns, are likewise personal. The prices at these markets for meat, seafood, dairy products, and produce are often lower than in the shops and the goods markedly fresher, two qualities that recommend themselves very highly to the French shopper. Flowers, candy, clothes, and an unpredictable assortment of other items also occupy the stalls. Many towns feature flea markets **(marchés aux puces),** which have much of the range and flavor of the American variety.

France offers large department stores **(grands magasins), Les Galeries Lafayette** and **Le Printemps** in Paris and **Les Nouvelles Galeries** outside Paris, with a wide range of merchandise presented stylishly. Chain stores that carry predictable, affordable ranges of clothes and variety goods, such as **Monoprix** and **Prisunic,** flourish in most French towns.

Paris holds numerous fashion shops with clothes by leading designers, and streets where they cluster, like the **rue du Faubourg Saint-Honoré,** attract many window-shoppers.

Shopping centers **(grandes surfaces)** are growing in popularity: near Versailles is **Parly 2** and **Créteil Soleil** is southeast of Paris, to name two. Also popular are the large **hypermarchés** (hypermarkets), which offer huge selections, cheap prices, ample parking, and late hours. French parsimony, impatience with city parking, and over-scheduled modern lives draw families to these expanses to push their laden cart **(le caddie)** to a long checkout line and then to the parking lot. Hypermarkets like **Auchan** in country areas are causing the closure of many local village shops just as they have in other countries.

❁

73. SPORTS

France has traditionally sought to lead the world more in intellectual than in athletic achievements. There are some signs of change. More French people are playing sports these days than formerly, a result of the recent focus on fitness **(la forme)** in news media and in society in general. The government has encouraged the trend with financing for recreation facilities such as swimming pools and sports fields. Although there is some level of enthusiasm for particular sports, sport in general is not integral in French life. Only one French person in five belongs to a sports club.

The French prefer individual to team sports and prefer the non-competitive among those. Skiing, swimming, and cycling are the most popular. In the South of France, open-air bowling and a type of bowling called **pétanque** are traditionally popular. Albertville in the French Alps has long been a popular ski area and was the site of the 1992 Winter Olympics. Huge crowds watch the **Tour de France** cycling race around the country in June and July, and the winner receives national acclaim.

Skiers come from all social classes. Tennis, sailing, and golf appeal mainly to the upper classes. The French tennis championships, played on clay courts at Roland-Garros in Paris, prior to the famous Wimbledon lawn tennis tournament in London, draw leading world players. French sailors, often from Brittany, have been among the leaders in around-the-world and transatlantic yacht races. In 1990 Florence Arthaud (1957–   ) became the first woman to win an ocean yachting race and established the record for a solo crossing of the Atlantic, nine days and twenty-one hours.

Young people today enjoy windsurfing, and a growing number of adventure-seekers enjoy underwater diving and hang-gliding. Car racing enthusiasts attend two major events, the 24 Hours at Le Mans and the Monaco rally. The French driver Alain Prost (1955–   ) was for many years a leader in the world Formula 1 championship.

The principal team sports are soccer and rugby. The national competition between soccer clubs has a large following of regional enthusiasts who come to Paris for the final match at the Parc des Princes. France is the host country for the international soccer World Cup in 1998.

Rugby is most popular in the Southwest. The French generally see the European rugby competition, **le Tournoi des Cinq Nations** (England, France, Ireland, Scotland, and Wales) as a contest in national pride.

English cricket and American baseball have not taken root in France.

The national daily newspaper *L'Équipe* reports sporting events and results for a large public. The majority of French people prefer this level of sports involvement, as spectators and armchair analysts.

✖

74. STREET NAMES AND ADDRESSES

Paris is a very pleasant city to walk in. A stroll through the districts **(arrondissements)** provides reminders of French history not only from the architecture of previous centuries but also from street names. Streets in many French cities and towns carry the names of famous historical figures and events as well as of famous writers, musicians, and artists. Some contemporary celebrities also are commemorated in street names.

The French city thus forms a cultural environment for its inhabitants. People may not recall a great deal about some of the events and people in the street names, but the signposts remind them of a glorious past upon which the France of today and tomorrow were built.

Americans accustomed to the predictable grid pattern and numbering of city streets are often disoriented by the fact that French streets do not follow a recognizable geometric pattern and are called by names, not numbers.

Some streets are named after saints. Tourists using a street directory should remember that all such street names beginning with **Saint** precede those beginning with **Sainte,** which in turn precede any beginning with **Saints. Rue Saint-Thomas** thus precedes **rue Sainte-Geneviève,** which precedes **rue Saints-Côme-et-Damien** in a directory. Another distinct feature of French addresses is the use of **bis** and **ter** to insert new addresses between adjacent numbers. Where in the English system two addresses between 125 and 126 would be styled 125A and 125B, the French would call them **125 bis** and **125 ter.** (French concert-goers, incidentally, will cry **bis** to encourage an encore, not ''Encore!'' The encore performance is similarly **un bis.**)

✖

75. TIME

The French have their own concept of punctuality. It is accepted behavior to arrive a little late for a personal appointment, and guests may arrive up to half an hour after the agreed time for a dinner at a home without causing irritation to their hosts. However, the many French who travel by train get to the station punctually because the French national railway system has an enviable reputation for its trains leaving and arriving on time.

The French tend to separate their lives into periods of work and periods of pleasure. Periods of pleasure have a certain sanctity, especially mealtimes. School and work allow for a two-hour lunch break, although now that workers travel greater distances to work many work places have reduced the lunch hour to one hour, especially in large urban areas. It is not possible to squeeze shopping into a lunch break in many country towns, since most shops will be closed for the same period, usually 12 noon to 2 PM.

Managers often work until 7 PM. This delays the evening meal-time, which frequently takes place during or after the nightly television news broadcast at 8 PM.

The annual month-long summer vacation breaks the year into two parts for workers. These parts are further broken by one- or two-week vacations in winter, often spent skiing, and the long week-ends of **Toussaint** (November 1) and **Pâques** (Easter). All French salaried workers are officially entitled to five weeks of annual paid vacation.

Foreigners visiting France are often favorably impressed by the French ability to work long hours while not neglecting relaxation and enjoyment.

The French calendar week begins on Monday rather than Sunday. The expressions **huit jours** (eight days) and **quinze jours** (fifteen days) mean "a week" and "a fortnight." The word **prochain** (next) used with a weekday does not mean "in the next week" as it does to some English speakers. For example, **vendredi prochain,** when spoken on a Wednesday, means the Friday two days away, not the Friday nine days away. Wednesday is a day off for primary school children and a half day for high school students; on the other hand, both at present will sit for classes for a half day on Saturday; this could change because there is a proposal to have no classes on Saturday and give pupils a full weekend.

❖

76. TRANSPORT

The French train system is extremely efficient and carries many passengers. French trains are renowned for their speed and punctuality. The government opened a **TGV (train à grande vitesse)** route between Paris and Lyon in 1981; the train covers the 500 km journey in two hours. **TGV** trains now also serve Toulouse, Brittany, and the North from Paris. The comfort and speed of the **TGV** make it very popular and a direct competitor of the internal airline **Air Inter.** The **TGV** technology was purchased for the Houston-Dallas-San Antonio line, which was a commercial triumph for French engineering.

Paris has six major train stations, each one serving a different region of the country. Trains from the **Gare de Lyon,** for example, go south to Marseilles, the **Côte d'Azur,** and Italy, while those from the **Gare de l'Est** serve Strasbourg and Germany.

The French aeronautical industry has also enjoyed international success. The Concorde first flew from Paris to Rio de Janeiro in 1976. Since then, the Concorde fleets of Air France and British Airways have flown several million passengers over the Atlantic. Many international aviation companies have bought the Airbus, which is manufactured in Toulouse.

The underground railways in Paris, Lyon, and Marseilles are called **le métro.** In Paris, travelers can reach all parts of the city quickly because of the frequency of the trains, the 293 stations, and the numerous points **(correspondances)** for changing lines. **Métro** travel is also very economical, especially with the discount books of tickets **(carnets de billets).** A traveler pays one price for any one journey, no matter how long, short, simple, or serpentine the route used.

A fast train system called the **RER (Réseau Express Régional),** which has links to the **métro,** has been extended to the newer outer suburbs of Paris.

A large fleet of barges **(péniches)** carries raw and manufactured materials on France's extensive network of rivers and canals. Some barges also carry foreign and French tourists for tours of the more scenic canals.

❁

77. URBAN AND RURAL LIFE

France has a population of more than 58 million but is one of the least densely populated countries in Europe (259 inhabitants per square mile), roughly half the density of Germany or of Italy—or, for that matter, of Switzerland, which has a much smaller proportion of inhabitable land. Because 90 percent of the French population live in urban or semiurban areas and 20 percent in the **Île de France** region around Paris, large areas of the diverse country landscape offer unspoiled vistas of fields, forests, valleys, and mountains.

The population has moved rapidly from the country to urban agglomerations since World War II. In 1946, 38 percent of the total work force were farmers; in 1994, 6 percent were. The suburbs **(la banlieue)** of major cities grew as the countryside emptied. This also means that many of today's urban residents are within a generation of one rural area or another and its traditions, and many contemporary Parisians identify themselves, for example, as **bretons** or **normands** rather than Parisians—that is, they continue to identify themselves with the region from which their family came.

The relatively sudden influx of people needed housing, as did immigrant workers who began to enter the country. Low-cost high-rise apartment buildings called **HLM (habitations à loyer modéré)** were erected in the suburbs with government financing. Low-income workers from the city have added to the suburban mushroom as rents rose in their old neighborhoods under the economic pressure of gentrification. The **HLM** buildings are now often socially deprived concentrations of people with high unemployment, especially among the young and the immigrants. The current pattern is for high-income earners to live in the city center and low-income earners in the suburbs.

Individual housing developments were built in the outer suburbs around the ''New Towns'' planned by government and urban architects to decrease inner-city overcrowding resulting from the baby-boomer population.

In the 1980s, government reforms gave greater power to regional councils and provincial cities began a new growth cycle as a result. Regional economic growth was also stimulated by managers and other workers who abandoned the stress of Parisian life in search of a higher quality of life. The **TGV** network has reduced the isolation of provincial cities by making travel between them and Paris faster. Thirty-five urban agglomerations outside Paris hold more than 100,000 people. The five largest are, in order, Lyon, Marseille, Lille, Bordeaux, and Toulouse.

In the very recent past, agriculture made the greatest contribution to France's wealth and a stout proportion of its people lived in villages, where conservatism and respect for tradition were the most valued habits of mind. Today the traditional rural society has been displaced by an urban one in which services contribute more than 50 percent of the gross national product and the wholesale changes of modernization had to be accepted in order to survive. France has made the accommodation, but farmers' demonstrations against European Union agricultural policies received widespread popular support although only 5 percent of France's current economy was at stake. The nationalist and conservative values of the rural society continue to exert an influence on the national psyche out of all proportion to the economic importance of that society.

❌

78. VACATIONS

The socialist **Front Populaire** government of 1936 introduced a law mandating two weeks of paid annual vacation **(congés payés)** for all salaried workers. The law is often cited in France as a watershed in the progress of the working class toward an improved lifestyle. The required vacation was increased to three weeks in 1956, to four in 1969, and to five in 1982. Many workers in special categories now receive six weeks of paid vacation every year. Germany is the only country in the world where the annual vacation is longer than in France.

Most French people take their vacations in August, and many industrial plants close for the month. The first wave of crowds leave Paris and the North of France after the National Holiday of July 14 and seek out the sun and beaches of the Mediterranean and Atlantic coasts. The second wave departs on August 1. On August 15 a third wave leaves on vacation while those who left in mid July throng home. During the last weekend in August all roads and trains from the South to the North groan with the crowds returning home. In September people resume their work or schooling and life returns to normal after the pause in national life for summer vacation.

Many people use their fifth and sixth weeks of vacation to go skiing in the winter or to take other short trips. Twenty-seven percent of French people take several vacations a year, while for other Europeans the figure is 19 percent.

Fifty-six percent of French people took their vacations away from home in 1991. Eighty-seven percent of these vacationed in France, of which half spent the time either at the home of relatives or friends or at their own vacation home. The main destinations were beaches and country locations where varied landscapes or cultural treasures were strong attractions. Summer arts festivals in many towns and historical sites in the South attracted many, as for example the theater festival in Avignon and the music festival in Aix-en-Provence, which also drew many foreign visitors.

Only 12 percent of French people (increasingly, these are the young people) spent their vacation outside France in 1991. The percentage is much higher in other northern European countries: 64 percent of the Dutch, 60 percent of the Germans. More than 30 percent of these French people went to Spain or Portugal. An increasing number of French people want their vacation to be more intelligent than idle sunbathing **(le bronzage idiot)** on the beach. The Club Méditerranée, which began in 1950 with resorts in France, has expanded its village concept to reach this audience by building sites at many exotic locations and by offering cultural and sports activities and opportunities for self-improvement at its facilities.

In 1991 the Germans, British, and Italians were the most numerous of the 52 million foreign tourists in France. Since the bicentenary of the French Revolution in 1989, France has welcomed more foreign visitors than any other country. The United States is second and Spain third.

79. WORK AND UNEMPLOYMENT

Until well into this century, France was largely a rural nation. When it moved quickly into the forefront of world technology in the thirty years after World War II, the French adapted to become a skilled and enterprising work force. High-tech industries **(industries de pointe)** flourished while a large and economically active working class maintained France's manufacturing and agricultural output.

Recent years have seen an increase in the numbers of white-collar professional and managerial workers **(les cadres).** A large number of educated upper-class women joined the many women from the lower classes who had always been in the work force. Every town reveals the widespread contribution of women to its work force in its child-care centers **(les crèches).** Women are particularly well represented in social-work professions, teaching (especially at the primary level), and administration.

The French devote a lot of energy to work and enjoy its economic benefits, and so the rise in unemployment **(le chômage)** caused by the recession and advancing computerization **(l'informatisation)** has proved traumatic for them. Surveys regularly report unemployment as the leading source of anxiety. The contrast of these times with the security of the postwar economic boom adds an edge to unemployment concerns. The government has lowered the legal retirement age to sixty, but still 25 percent of those under twenty-five are out of work. Automation and computerization have decimated workers in unskilled and semiskilled manufacturing jobs, many of which immigrant workers used to fill. Managerial classes are also experiencing a rise in unemployment.

The specter of joining the unemployment lines at the **ANPE (Agence Nationale pour l'Emploi)** has affected French attitudes toward education, and parents have begun to demand that their children learn employable skills as well as the traditional intellectual skills.

Unemployment has brought political disillusion and a swing to the right. The extreme right has begun to sound convincing when it claims that fewer foreign-born workers would translate to more jobs for the French. French foreign policy has also reacted to unemployment as farmers and fishermen protest regularly about cheap imports that threaten their jobs. In short, the justified fear of unemployment has reinforced the traditional tendency toward individualism and nationalism in French social behavior.

❁

80. WORLD WARS AND COLONIAL WARS

Germany declared war on France on August 3, 1914. World War I developed into a trench war (1915–17) between the combined French and Allied forces and the German army in the North of France. The French won the Battle of Verdun in 1916, but only after suffering severe losses of human life. An armistice was signed on November 11, 1918, after American forces had joined the Allied forces. One quarter of the young French males had died in the war (nearly 1.5 million French soldiers died in all), and this restricted greatly both France's economic recovery and its population growth for decades.

Germany under Hitler was again at war with France in 1939, when World War II began. In 1940 the French army collapsed before the German tank offensive and, on June 25, the eighty-four-year-old Marshal Philippe Pétain (1856–1951), the new leader of the French government, signed an armistice with Germany. The Nazi army occupied outright the entire North of France and the Atlantic coastline while the South was given nominal independence with its capital at Vichy. General Charles de Gaulle (1890–1970) had broadcast a patriotic call from London on June 18 urging the French not to collaborate with the Nazis because "France has lost a battle! But France has not lost the war!" He organized the Free French movement outside of France. Jean Moulin (1899–1943) and others organized the French Resistance movement within Vichy France. On D-Day, June 6, 1944, Allied forces made up of 1.7 million British, 1.5 million Americans, and 220,000 soldiers of other nationalities under the command of General Dwight D. Eisenhower landed on the coast of Normandy to liberate France. Paris was liberated on August 25, 1944, and the war in Europe ended on May 8, 1945. General de Gaulle and those in the Resistance were the war heroes and Marshal Pétain was condemned to prison for treason. Other major Vichy collaborators were summarily executed or imprisoned after court trials. Some notorious war criminals were not convicted, because of an ambivalent attitude among many French about Vichy policies.

In 1946 France became embroiled in a war for independence in its colony of Indochina. The Vietminh forces attacked a French army in 1954 at Dien Bien Phu and inflicted a humiliating defeat on it, forcing France to withdraw from Vietnam.

The same year that France accepted defeat in Vietnam, the North African French territory of Algeria began a war for its independence. Two other French colonies in North Africa, Morocco and Tunisia, had been granted independence without contest, but Algeria had not. Algeria was unique among French colonies in having been integrated into the administrative structure of mainland France, and a significant part of the population was French. It was difficult for the army and indeed for much of mainland France to accept an independent Algeria. In 1958 President René Coty (1882–1962), fearing a civil war between supporters of a French Algeria and supporters of an independent Algeria, recalled General de Gaulle to form a new French government. De Gaulle first granted independence to all other French African colonies who wished for it and then negotiated a cease-fire between the French army and the forces for independent Algeria. In 1962, Algeria received its independence.

France had endured seventeen years of colonial war after World War II and was finally at peace. The baby-boomer generation began entering the work force to fill the gap created by the dead of World War I, and France earnestly began to expand its economy, which brought improvements in its standard of living.

❁

81. X

X is the colloquial name for the **École Polytechnique** founded in 1794 as a school for engineers of public works. In 1804, Napoleon Bonaparte (1769–1821) gave it the status of a military school, which it still retains. The students wore a uniform and a two-cornered hat. Women were first allowed to enroll in 1972. X and the **École Nationale d'Administration (ENA)**, founded in 1945, are the most prestigious higher education institutions, and their graduates readily find appointment to the top ranks of industry and the civil service. These two form the elite among the prestigious **Grandes Écoles,** and students gain admittance to them by their performance on a very difficult competitive examination that, in the case of **X,** consists primarily of advanced mathematics and physics.

82. XENOPHOBIA

One of the main reasons the extreme-right-wing National Front Party led by Jean-Marie Le Pen (1928–   ) became relatively popular in the 1980s was its anti–Arab immigrant policy. The party received a surprising 11 percent of the French vote in the 1984 European elections, and Le Pen himself got 14.4 percent of the vote in France's 1988 presidential election. Some unemployed workers who had been used to voting communist had contributed to Le Pen's results, as had former supporters of other conservative parties who were disappointed in the feebleness of their parties' defense of the French identity of France.

Le Pen's theme ''France for the French'' found a receptive audience among the growing ranks of the unemployed and those who were afraid of joining their ranks during the recession.

Le Pen and his supporters blamed Arab immigrants for working in jobs that unemployed French workers could fill. They conveniently forgot that these jobs went begging until the Arabs arrived to do them. They attacked as un-French the immigrants' continued practice of their Muslim religion.

The **Beurs,** that is, children of Arab and African immigrants living in France, founded an antiracist association called SOS-Racisme with socialist encouragement. SOS-Racisme organized concerts that attracted large crowds of young people who opposed Le Pen's racist campaign. The association's emblem was the open hand of friendship with the slangy slogan **Touche pas à mon pote** (Hands off my pal).

In 1993 the conservative government began taking a harder line against illegal immigration and tightened qualifications for French citizenship, which eroded the appeal of the National Front. Tensions remain, however. The Islamic fundamentalist movement has spread to Algeria, where it has taken the form of the Islamic Salvation Front, and its influence extends to Algerians working in France. Their activities exacerbate the racist attitudes of the extremists in the French population.

❈

83. YÉYÉ

In the 1960s young French pop singers introduced a new wave of music called **yéyé** to the young generation born after World War II. The young people had become a large group in the population by this time and followed their own styles and tastes, which often shocked the conservative older generations. The **yéyé** songs, often adaptations of American and British rock and pop songs, were the first inroads of international pop culture into France. The name **yéyé** came from the ''yeah, yeah'' that was heard in popular music such as that performed by the famous British group The Beatles and other American and British groups. The most popular **yéyé** singers were Johnny Halliday (1943–   ), Eddy Mitchell (1942–   ), Sylvie Vartan (1944–   ), and Françoise Hardy (1944–   ).

This Anglo-Saxon-inspired pop culture that catered to an expanding youth market developed even as other artists were perfecting the French poetic song, in which emotions were expressed through images evoked by crafted word combinations with a simple guitar or piano accompaniment. The poetic songs of Georges Brassens (1921–81), Leo Ferré (1916–93), Jacques Brel (1929–78), and Barbara (1930–) continue to have popularity today. The love songs of Édith Piaf (1915–63), of a style popular a generation earlier, also continue to find a following.

The government guarantees French artists an audience and protects the integrity of French national culture by requiring that at least 40 percent of the songs a radio station plays must be French.

❈

84. ZAPPING

Zapping between television programs allows viewers to exercise some individual control over what images enter their homes through the screen. The French also apply **le zapping** to a new tendency in French behavior, to shift rapidly from brand to brand, in attitude, between jobs, or from one romantic partner to another.

The French now enjoy greater professional mobility and French individuals now have more contact with social and regional groups outside their own. The progress of the European Union has introduced into France the values and behaviors of other European countries. Economic issues have become global through the activities of multinational corporations, and France as the fourth-largest exporter in international trade has become very aware of world trends and concerns. All these developments make for an unsettling perspective for the younger French generation, who zap from one fashion to another and are keener to travel and make friends than the older generation.

The increased choices of a consumer society, more sophisticated advertising techniques, the weakening of traditional values, wider cultural experience—each of these is a partial explanation for the emergence of zapping as a feature of French behavior.

❁

85. *ZUT!*

This frequent French exclamation, which often becomes **Zut, alors!**, expresses frustration and exasperation. It is a polite expression used by all social groups, whereas the somewhat equivalent **Merde!** is considered impolite.

The exclamation **Bof!** expresses indifference to an idea or project. If a French person replies **Bof!** with a shrug of the shoulders to a proposal, you know not to expect any enthusiasm. **Super!** or **Génial!** expresses an enthusiastic response.

BIBLIOGRAPHY

Ardagh, J. *France Today* (London, Eng.: Penguin, 1990).

Flower, J. E., ed. *France Today* (London, Eng.: Hodder & Stoughton, 1993).

Frears, J. R. *France in the Giscard Presidency* (London, Eng.: Allen & Unwin, 1981).

Hanley, D. L., A. P. Kerr, and N. H. Waites, *Contemporary France* (London, Eng.: Routledge & Kegan Paul, 1984).

McMillan, J. F. *Twentieth Century France: Politics and Society 1898–1991* (London, Eng.: Edward Arnold, 1992).

Pickles, D. *Problems of Contemporary French Politics* (London, Eng.: Methuen, 1982).

Scriven, M., and P. Wagstaff, eds. *War and Society in Twentieth Century France* (New York: Berg, 1991).

Slater, M. *Contemporary French Politics* (London, Eng.: Macmillan, 1985).

Tint, H. *France since 1918* (London, Eng.: Batsford, 1980).

Werth, A. *De Gaulle: A Political Biography* (London, Eng.: Penguin, 1969)

Wright, G. *France in Modern Times* (New York: Norton, 1981).

ABOUT THE AUTHOR

Ross Steele has published extensively on contemporary France, on the French newsmagazine *L'Express,* and on the teaching of French culture.

He teaches at the University of Sydney, Australia, and is an Adjunct Senior Fellow of the National Foreign Language Center in Washington, D.C.

He has been honored with two awards by the government of France for international promotion of French language and culture: *Officier de l'Ordre National du Mérite* and *Officier des Palmes Académiques.*

INDEX

A

abbreviations and acronyms 1–3
Abélard 53
Académie française 3, 4
accents and language 3–5
acronyms 1
addresses 81, 82
aerobics 42
African colonies 68, 89–90
African immigrants 51, 91
Age of Enlightenment 17, 56, 76, 78
agriculture 51, 85–86
AIDS 3, 41
Airbus 44, 84
Air France 84
Air Inter 83
Aix-en-Provence 87
Algeria 34, 51–52, 89–91
Allied forces 38, 88–89
Alsace 22, 34, 75, 77
Americanization 3–4
American Revolution 43
amis 31
amour 52
Ancien Régime 76
anciens francs 63
Anglo-Saxon 6, 18, 39, 92
animals 5
anniversaire 64
ANPE 2, 88
antisemitism 76
apartments 7, 48–49

apéritif 22
Arabs 51–52, 90–91
Arc de Triomphe 70
Ariane rocket 44
aristocracy 54, 76
Armistice Day 48, 88
arrondissements 81
Arthaud, Florence (1957–) 81
Ascension Day 47
Asnières 7
asperges 59
Assumption Day 47–48
Astérix 50
automobile manufacturing 51
automobiles 21, 22–23, 65
autoroutes 23
Avignon 10, 87

B

baby-boomer 85, 90
baccalauréat 25, 57
Baccarat crystal 15
baguette 10
baiser 54
Balladur, Edouard (1929–) 9, 26, 38
bandes dessinées (BD) 3, 50
banlieue 69, 85
Barbara (1930–) 92
Bardot, Brigitte (1934–) 7, 43
Bastille 43, 47, 76
Beaubourg museum 19
Beaujolais wine 21

INDEX

Beauvoir, Simone de (1908–86) 53
beaux quartiers 71
Bébête show Le 51
Becquerel, Henri 43
Belleville 71
Bénézet, Saint 10
Berlioz, Hector (1803–69) 19
Bernadette, Saint (1844–79) 75
Beurs 52, 91
bicentenary 15, 69, 87
biftek frites 59
biotechnology 44
bis 82
blanquette de veau 59
Bleu-Blanc-Rouge 7
Bleus, les 7
Bocuse, Paul (1926–) 34
bof 93
bon appétit 72
Bordeaux 85
Bordeaux wine 21, 34
boudin blanc 59
bouillabaisse 34, 59
boulangerie 9–10, 79
Boulevard Périphérique 69
bourgeoisie 8–9, 54, 64
boutiques 79
Brassens, Georges (1921–81) 92
bread 9–10, 59–60
Brel, Jacques (1929–78) 92
Bresse 34
bridges 10–11, 49
Brittany 83
bronzage idiot 87
Brussels 27
bûche de Noël 48
Burgundy 73
Burgundy wine 21
business practices 11–13, 18

C

caddie 80
cadres 87
Caesar, Julius 42
cafés 13–14, 33
Cahiers du Cinéma, Les 16
calling cards 14–15
Camargue 23
Cameroun 68

Canal-Plus 60
Canard enchaîné, Le 51
can-can 53
Cannes Film Festival 15
car, le 28
Cardin, Pierre (1922–) 30
Carême, Marie-Antoine (1784–1833) 34
Carnet du jour, Le 15
carnets de billets 84
carnival 46
Carte Bleue 63
carte d'allocations familiales 21
carte de sécurité sociale 21
carte grise 21
carte nationale d'identité 20
cartes de visite 14
Cartesian logic 56
Cartier 15
casinos 33
cassoulet 34
cave 21
centime 63
Cévennes 23
Chambord Castle 18
champagne 15, 21
Champs-Élysées 69
Chandeleur 46
Chanel, Coco (1883–1971) 30
Channel Tunnel 11, 74
charcuterie 79
chauvinism 90–91
Chevalier, Maurice (1888–1972) 10
Chirac, Jacques (1932–) 26, 70
choucroute 34
Christianity 74–75
chrysanthemums 31, 48
cinema 15–16
Citroën 22
Clair, René (1898–1981) 16
clochards 49
Clovis 74
Coca-Cola 5, 22
Cocorico! 16–17
code de la porte 49
Cognac 34
cohabitation 38
collaboration 38, 89
colonial wars 88–90
colonies 68, 88–90

Coluche (1944–86) 49
commissariat de police 35
Common Market 26
commune 38, 73
commune de Paris 70, 77
Communist party 8
concentration camps 76
concierge 49
Concorde 84
Condé, prince de (1621–86) 33
condition féminine 62
congés payés 86
Congo 68
connaissances 31
conseillers 38
Constitution 77–78
constitutional monarchy 77
contraception 62
contrôle d'identité 35
conversation 17–18
coq au vin 59
coq gaulois 16–17
Corsica 24, 68
Côte d'Azur 84
Côte d'Ivoire 68
Coty, René (1882–1962) 90
couscous 34
Cousteau, Jacques (1910–) 24
credit cards 63
crêpes 46
Cresson, Édith (1934–) 38, 62
Créteil Soleil 80
CRS 3, 35
cuisine minceur 34
cultural tourism 18–19
culture 19–20
Curie, Marie (1867–1934) and Pierre
    (1859–1906) 43
Cyrano de Bergerac 43

D

Daguerre, Louis-Jacques (1787–1851) 55–56
D-Day 89
débrouillardise 73
decentralization 70, 74
Declaration of the Rights of Man and of the
    Citizen 37, 76, 78
decorations 20
Défense, La 70

déjeuner 59
Delors, Jacques (1925–) 27
demonstrations 35–36
Deneuve, Catherine (1943–) 16, 43
Dépardieu, Gérard (1948–) 16
départements 65, 68, 73
départements d'outre-mer 68
Descartes, René (1596–1650) 56
designer goods 15
Dien Bien Phu 87
diet 42, 54
digestif 22
Dijon 34
dîner 59
Dior, Christian (1905–57) 30
directness 12, 71
divorce 29, 57–58, 62
documents and forms 20–21, 78–79
DOM 68
Dreyfus, Alfred (1859–1935) 76
drinking 21–22
driving 22–23

E

eau minérale 21
École des Hautes Études Commerciales 12
École Nationale d'Administration 12, 26,
    90
École Polytechnique 12, 26, 90
ecology 23–24
economy 44, 92
écu 2, 63
EDF 2
Nantes, Edict of 75
education 24–26, 88, 90
Eiffel Tower 43
Eisenhower, Dwight D. (1890–1969) 89
s'embrasser 54
Emmaüs 49
empire 77
ENA 12, 26, 90
énarques 26
endives 59
épargne 63
épicerie 79
Epiphany 46
Équipe, L' 81
Escoffier, Auguste (1846–1935) 34
esprit 50

INDEX

etiquette 39, 54
Eureka 44
Euro Disneyland 5
Euro-jargon 26
Europe 26–28
Europe 1 radio station 61
European coal and steel 26
European Economic Community 2, 26, 74
European Parliament 27, 37
European Space Consortium 44
European Union 2, 27, 52, 63, 86, 92
Euro Tunnel 11, 74
Évenement du jeudi, L' 61
Évian 22
exams 25
Express, L' 61
extra 28
extreme right 38, 52, 88

F

Fabius, Laurent (1946–) 26
faire-part 14
family 29
farewells 39–41
fashion 29–30
Faubourg St-Honoré 80
Fayette, marquis de la (1757–1834) 43
Ferré, Léo (1916–93) 92
fête 64
Fête du Travail 31, 47
feuilletons 60
fève 46
Figaro, Le 8, 15, 61
fishing 55
fitness 41–42
fleur de lys 7
flippers 14
flowers and gardens 31
foie gras 32
Folies Bergère 53
foot 28
forme 80
Foundation for Animal Protection 7
franc 63
France d'outre-mer 68
France métropolitaine 68
Franco-Prussian War 70
franglais 4
Free French Movement 43, 89

French Republic. *See* Republic
French Revolution. *See* Revolution
friendship 31–32
frogs and snails, garlic and truffles 32
Front Populaire 86

G

Gabon 68
galette des rois 46
gambling 32–33
gardens 31
gardien/gardiennes 49
Gare de Lyon 84
Gargantua 50
garlic 32
gastronomy 33–35
GATT 2, 6, 27
Gaul 19, 50
Gaulle, Charles de (1890–1970) 26, 28, 34,
    37, 38–39, 43, 63, 68, 73, 77, 89–90
Gaultier, Jean-Paul (1952–) 30
gendarmes 35–36
Génération Écologie 24
génial 93
gens bien 9
German invasions 38, 76, 77, 89
gestures 36–37
Giroud, Françoise 62
Giscard d'Estaing, Valéry (1926–) 26, 65
Giverny, Normandy 31
golden boys 64
Gothic cathedrals 74
goûter 59
Goutte d'Or 71
government 37–38
Grande Arche 70
Grandes Écoles 12, 25, 90
grandes surfaces 80
grandeur 38–39, 43
grands magasins 79
Greens 24, 38
greetings 39–40
Guadeloupe 68
Guide Culinaire 34
Guignols de l'Info 51
guillotine 41
Guinée 68
Guyane française 68

H

Halliday, Johnny (1943–) 92
Hardy, Françoise (1944–) 92
haute couture 30
health and fitness 41–42
Héloïse 53
Hermès 15
heroes and heroines 42
Heure de Verité, L' 61
Hexagone 44
hexagonal attitude 44
high tech 44, 46
HLM 3, 49, 85
holidays 31, 46–49
homeopathic 42
hors d'oeuvre 22, 32, 59
housing 48–49, 71, 85
Huguenots 75
Humanité, L' 61
humor 50–51
hunting 55

I

Île de France 84
Île de la Cité 69
immigration 51–52, 91
Indochina 89
industries de pointe 87
informatisation 88
intellectuals 57
Islam 75

J

jardin à la française 31
je me souviens 7
je t'aime 52
Jews 76
joaillerie 79
Joan of Arc 42
jogging 42
joie de vivre 53
Jour de l'An 47
July 14 47, 59, 76, 86

K

kilos 53–54
kir 22
kissing 39, 54

L

laïcité 75
language 3–5, 54
Lanvin, Jean (1867–1946) 30
lapin 59
Latin Quarter 69
Légion d'honneur 20
leisure 53, 55–56
letters 40–41
Libération 61
liberté, égalité, fraternité 56, 78
librairie 79
Lille 85
line, waiting in 72–73
livret de famille 20, 57
logic 56–57
Loto 33
Louis XIV (1638–1715) 33, 43, 75
Louis XV (1710–74) 17
Louis XVI (1754–93) 41
Louvre museum 15, 18, 19, 31, 69
Lumière, Auguste (1862–1954) and Louis
    (1864–1948) 15–16
Luxembourg Gardens 31
luxury goods 15
Lyon 74, 83–85

M

Maastricht Treaty 28
madeleine 10
mairie 21, 57, 62
Mali 68
Malle, Louis (1932–) 16
manifestations 35
Mans, Le 81
Marceau, Sophie (1966–) 43
marchés 79–80
Mardi Gras 46
Marianne 43, 62
Marie-Antoinette (1755–93) 9, 41
markets 79–80
marriage 57–58
''Marseillaise, La'' 58–59
Marseilles 58, 84
Martinique 68
May 1968 24, 77
Mayotte 69
meals 59–60

media 55, 57, 60–61
Médicis, Marie de (1573–1642) 33, 35
men and women 61–62
metric system 53–54
métro 69, 84
Michelin guidebooks 18, 33
Milou 50
Minitel 44
Miquelon 69
Mitchell, Eddy (1942–) 92
Mitterrand, François (1916–) 9, 28, 37, 41, 62, 73
Molière (1622–73) 35
Monde, Le 61
Monet, Claude (1840–1926) 31
money 63–64
Monnet, Jean (1888–1979) 26
Montagnier, Luc (1932–) 41
Montaigne, Michel de (1533–92) 55
Mont Blanc Tunnel 11
Monte Carlo rally 23, 81
Montesquieu (1689–1755) 76
Montmartre 69
Montparnasse 69
Moreno, Roland (1945–) 46
Morocco 89
Moulin, Jean (1899–1943) 89
muguet 31, 47
municipal council 38, 73
Muslims 75, 91

N

names and name days 64
Napoleon Bonaparte (1769–1821) 20, 32, 43, 64, 77, 90
Napoleon III (1808–73) 30, 77
national anthem 58–59
National Assembly 37, 68–69
National Day 47, 59, 86
National Front party 52, 90
Nazis 38, 76, 89
New Look 30
Nice 46
Niepce, Nicéphore (1765–1833) 55
Niger 68
Noël 48
Normandie, pont de 11
Nôtre, André, Le (1613–1700) 31
Notre-Dame de Paris 69

Nouvelle Calédonie, La 69
nouvelle cuisine 34
Nouvel Observateur, Le 61
nuclear power 24
numbers 65, 68

O

Olivier, Michel (1932–) 34
Ordre des Arts et des Lettres 20
Ordre des Palmes Académiques 20
Ordre National du Mérite 20
Orsay museum 18, 19, 69
Overseas Departments and Territories 68–69

P

pain 10
Palme d'Or 15
Pantagruel 50
Pâques 47, 83
pardon 72
Paris 29–30, 69–71, 73–74, 79–80, 83–85
Parisians 70–71, 85
Paris to Dakar Rally 24
Parliament 78
Parly 2 80
Pasteur, Louis (1822–95) 22, 41
pastis 22
pastry 9–10
pâté de foie gras 48
Patou, Jean (1880–1936) 30
peasants 63, 76
Pei, I. M. (1917–) 15
Pen, Jean-Marie le (1928–) 90–91
péniches 84
Pentecost 47
Père Noël 48
perfide Albion 6
Périgord 19
permis de conduire 21
Perrier 21
Pétain, Philippe (1856–1951) 38, 89
pétanque 80
petit déjeuner 59
Peugeot 22
photography 55
Piaf, Edith (1915–63) 92
Picasso, Pablo (1881–1973) 19
Picasso Museum 19
Pierre, abbé (1912–) 49
Pigalle 53

Place de la Concorde 41, 70
PMU 3, 33
Point, Le 61
Poiret, Paul (1879–1944) 30
poisson d'avril 46–47
politeness and directness 71–72
politics 37–38, 51
Polynésie française 69
Pompadour, Marquise de (1721–64) 17
Pompidou Center 19, 69
Pont Neuf 10
porte-bonheur 31
pot au feu 59
poulet frites 59
pourboire 14
préfet/préfète 73
president 37, 70, 78
prime minister 37, 62
profiteroles 10
Prost, Alain (1955–) 81
Proust, Marcel (1871–1922) 10
provinces 73
Pyrénées 23

Q

quarté 33
quatorze juillet 47, 59, 76, 86
Québec 4, 7
queues 72
quinté 33

R

Rabelais (c. 1494–1553) 50
racing 81
radio 61
raisonnable 56
rationalism 56
recession 38, 49, 52, 64, 88, 91
regionalization 72–73
réligieuse 10
religion 46–48, 58, 74–75
Renault, Louis (1877–1944) 22
Renoir, Jean (1894–1979) 16
Republic 17, 37, 56, 65, 75–77
RER 1, 84
résidence secondaire 49
Resistance 43, 89
restaurants 13, 33–34
Réunion 68

réveillon 48
Revolution 7, 9, 17, 41, 43, 51, 53, 56, 75, 77, 78
Rheims 21
rights 78–79
Robuchon, Joël (1945–) 34
Rocard, Michel (1930–) 26
Rodin, Auguste (1840–1917) 19
Roland-Garros 81
Rome, Treaty of 26
Roquefort 34
Rostand, Edmond (1868–1918) 43
Rouget de Lisle (1760–1836) 58
rural life 7, 84–86

S

Saint-Laurent, Yves (1936–) 30
Saint-Michel, abbey of 18
Saint-Pierre 69
saint's day 64
Saint-Sylvestre 47
sandwich 10
santé 41
Sartre, Jean-Paul (1905–80) 53
satellite television 44, 60
Schumann, Robert (1886–1963) 26
SDF 3, 49
Seine 69
Sénégal 4, 23, 68
shopping 78–79, 82
silverware 60
Singer sewing machine 30
smart card 46
snails 32
social class 8–9, 24–25, 33, 49, 62, 63, 71, 76–77, 80–81, 85–88
Socialist party 9, 37, 73, 91
social security 42, 58
Sorbonne 31
SOS-Racisme 91
"Sous les Ponts de Paris" 10
spa 42
sports 55, 79–81, 87
Spot land observation satellite 44
Strasbourg 26, 58
street names and addresses 81
super 93
"Sur le Pont d'Avignon" 10
système D 73

INDEX

T

table manners 60
Tancarville, pont de 11
Tapie, Bernard (1945–) 64
tarte tatin 10
Tchad 68
technology 44–45
Télé 7 Jours 61
telecommunications 44–45
television 33, 34, 42, 55, 60, 92
ter 82
territories 68–69
TGV 1, 11, 44, 74, 83, 85
three stars 33
tiercé 33
time 82–83
Tintin 50
Togo 68
TOM 68
Toulouse 74, 83, 85
Tour de France 80
tourism 5, 18–19, 33, 69, 72
Toussaint 31, 48
trade union 8, 47
trains 82, 84, 86
transport 83–84
trente glorieuses, les 8
tricolore 7
Truffaut, François (1932–84) 16
truffles 32
tu 31
Tuileries Gardens 31
Tunisia 51–52, 89
tunnels 10–11

U

unemployment 38, 49, 52, 85, 87–88
urban and rural life 84–86

V

vacations 29, 83, 85–86
VAL 1, 44

Varda, Agnès (1928–) 16
Vartan, Sylvie (1944–) 92
Vatel 33
Veil, Simone (1927–) 27, 62
Vercingetorix 42, 50
Verdun 88
Versailles Palace 18, 31
Verts 24
Vichy regime 38, 51, 89
Vichy water 42
Vietnam 51, 89
vin de table 21
Vincent de Paul (1581–1660) 75
Vionnet, Madeleine (1876–1975) 30
Voltaire (1694–1778) 56
vous 32, 40

W

Wallis-et-Futuna 69
war criminals 89
Wars of Religion 75
Washington, George (1732–99) 43, 76
Winter Olympics 80
women 61–62
work 85–88
World Cup (soccer) 81
World Exhibition 43
World War I 77, 88–89
World War II 5, 77, 85, 87, 89, 91
world wars and colonial wars 88–90
Worth, Charles (1825–95) 30

X

X 12, 90
xenophobia 90–91

Y

Yalta Conference 39
yéyé 91

Z

zapping 91–92
zut 92